LIVING THE LETTERS
Ephesians

LIVING THE LETTERS
Ephesians

A NavStudy Featuring

NAVPRESS®

BRINGING TRUTH TO LIFE

OUR GUARANTEE TO YOU

We believe so strongly in the message of our books that we are making this quality guarantee to you. If for any reason you are disappointed with the content of this book, return the title page to us with your name and address and we will refund to you the list price of the book. To help us serve you better, please briefly describe why you were disappointed. Mail your refund request to: NavPress, P.O. Box 35002, Colorado Springs, CO 80935.

The Navigators is an international Christian organization. Our mission is to advance the gospel of Jesus and His kingdom into the nations through spiritual generations of laborers living and discipling among the lost. We see a vital movement of the gospel, fueled by prevailing prayer, flowing freely through relational networks and out into the nations where workers for the kingdom are next door to everywhere.

NavPress is the publishing ministry of The Navigators. The mission of NavPress is to reach, disciple, and equip people to know Christ and make Him known by publishing life-related materials that are biblically rooted and culturally relevant. Our vision is to stimulate spiritual transformation through every product we publish.

ISBN-13: 978-1-60006-030-4
ISBN-10: 1-60006-030-7

Cover design by Disciple Design
Cover photo by Phillip Parker
Creative Team: Terry Behimer, Brad Lewis, Amy Spencer, Reagen Reed, Arvid Wallen, Pat Reinheimer

Written and compiled by John Blase

Some of the anecdotal illustrations in this book are true to life and are included with the permission of the persons involved. All other illustrations are composites of real situations, and any resemblance to people living or dead is coincidental.

All Scripture quotations in this publication are taken from *THE MESSAGE* (MSG). Copyright © 1993, 1994, 1995, 1996, 2000, 2001, 2002. *THE MESSAGE* Numbered Edition copyright © 2005. Used by permission of NavPress Publishing Group.

Printed in the United States

1 2 3 4 5 6 7 8 9 10 / 10 09 08 07

CONTENTS

ABOUT THE
LIVING THE LETTERS
SERIES

Letters take time to write, usually much more time
than talk. They require a certain level of artfulness and
thoughtfulness in expression. Then they remain, to be reread,
perhaps to be stored away for another day of reading, or
even to be encountered some distant time by a future,
unknown eavesdropper. All of these aspects of the letter
invite soulfulness: rereading is a form of reflective meditation;
keeping letters honors memory and not only daily living;
and speaking to a reader not yet present in this life
respects the soul's eternal nature.
—THOMAS MOORE, *SOUL MATES*

This isn't your typical Bible study. You won't find any blanks to fill in,
questions with obvious answers, or maps of Paul's missionary journeys.

So what is *it*? That's a good question. Think of this book as an
opportunity. It's a chance to allow God's Spirit to speak to you in a way
that he's done for centuries—through letters.

Unfortunately, we live in a time when many consider e-mail a form
of letter writing. Every once in a while, it might be. But usually it's not.
Think about it: E-mail is often written quickly and absentmindedly.
How many times have you clicked *send* and then thought, *Oh, no!*

As Moore points out in the above quote, letter writing takes time.
Letter reading does too. So you can view this as an opportunity to add
time to your day or at least to spend what time you have in a worthy
manner.

This collection of paper and ink takes Paul's letter to the Ephesians and surrounds it with letters and journal entries from others in history who seemed to be trying to invite some of the same *reflective meditation*. Please understand that this isn't a subtle attempt to equate a letter or journal entry of Samuel Rutherford with the divinely inspired letter written by Paul. If anything, it's an attempt to underscore the timeless quality of God's correspondence with humanity—and to be aware of God speaking in a letter written by Garrison Keillor or by your Aunt Sue.

Briefly, each lesson includes an entry from Paul's letter to the Ephesians (using Eugene Peterson's *The Message*), followed by several other "letters" and a poem from contemporary writers. The challenge is to read and reread these letters. Come back and read them again days or weeks later. Questions and statements along the way will challenge you to engage the words on the page, prodding your heart, mind, soul, and strength. Yet don't approach any of this quickly or absentmindedly; rather, aim to live over and over again what you read and learn.

In so doing, might your life resemble something meditative, memorable, and eternal. *Live the letters.*

HOW TO APPROACH
LIVING THE LETTERS

This NavStudy is meant to be completed on your own and in a small group. You'll want to line up your reflection group (or whatever you want to call it) ahead of time. A group of four to six is optimal—any larger, and one or more members will likely be shut out of discussions. Your group can also be as small as two. Each person will need his or her own copy of this book.

Lessons follow the rhythm of *lectio divina,* the ancient practice of *divine reading.* The four movements are the ingredients of a spiritual frame of mind: (1) *Read*—the recitation of a short text of Scripture; (2) *Think*—an effort to wrestle with the meaning of a passage and make it personally relevant; (3) *Pray*—responding to the text and asking for God's grace in doing so; and (4) *Live*—experiencing God's love and his will for you. Divine reading has also been described in this way: Reading lies on the surface, thinking moves to the inner substance, praying involves voicing the desire, and living is the experience.

For each lesson in this book, use the four movements as follows:

1. *Read* the Scripture passage and the other readings in each section. Let them soak in. Saturate your heart, mind, soul, and strength. Reread if necessary. There's no blue ribbon for finishing quickly. Make notes in the white space on the page. If you like journaling, think of this as a space to journal.

2. *Think* about what you read. Take your time and respond to the questions provided. In addition to the questions, always ask, "What does this mean?" and "Why does this matter?" about the readings. Use your reflections to generate discussion with the other people in your group. Allow the experience of others to broaden your wisdom. You'll definitely be stretched—called on to evaluate what you've discovered

and asked to make practical sense of it. In community, this stretching can often be painful and sometimes even embarrassing. However, your willingness to be transparent—your openness to the possibility of personal growth—will reap great rewards.

3. *Pray.* That sounds so easy, doesn't it? But we all know it's not. In each lesson, read the poem provided and let God's Spirit cause words and phrases to stand out and be combined with the thoughts from the readings. Then allow that combination to be your prayer. It won't sound like a regular prayer; in fact, let this time expand your usual practice of prayer. At times, you might not be able to voice your thoughts aloud. Remember, the Spirit intercedes for us, interpreting even our "groans" to the Father.

4. *Live.* *Live* as in rhymes with *give.* How can you live out the thoughts, feelings, emotions, truths, challenges, and confessions you've experienced in the lesson? Each lesson will encourage you to write a letter to yourself. When your group gets together, talk over these letters. Commit to living out what you express in your letter, and ask your small group to hold you accountable with prayer and support.

Chapter 1 - next week

After going through each week's lesson on your own, sit down with a few other people and go deeper. Here are a few thoughts on how to make the most of that time.

Set ground rules. You don't need many. Here are two:

First, you'll want to commit, as a group, to see this through to completion. Significant personal growth happens when group members spend enough time together to really get to know each other. It doesn't have to be every week, but you do need to establish some element of consistency to your time together.

Second, agree together that everyone's story is important. Time is probably the most valuable commodity today, so if you have just an hour to spend together, do your best to give each person ample time to express concerns, pass along insights, and feel like a participating member of the group. Small-group discussions aren't monologues; however, a one-person-dominated discussion isn't always a bad thing either. Not only is your role in a small group to explore and expand your own understanding, it's also to support one another. If one group member truly needs more of the floor, give it to that person. There will be times when the needs of the one outweigh the needs of the many. Use good judgment and allow extra space when needed; *your* time might be the next time your group meets.

Meet regularly. Choose a time and place, and stick to it. Don't be surprised if this becomes a struggle. Go into this study with that expectation and push through it.

Let God lead. Each time you get together, guess who else is in the room? That's right—God. Be sensitive to how he is leading. Does your time need to be structured? If so, following the book's structure is a good idea. Does the time need breathing room instead? Then take a breath, step back, and see what God does.

Talk openly. You'll all be a little tentative at first. You're not a bad person if you're hesitant to unpack all your *stuff* in front of friends or new acquaintances. Maybe you're just a little skeptical about the value of revealing to others the deepest parts of who you are. Maybe you're simply too afraid of what those revelations might sound or look like. Discomfort isn't the goal; rather, the goal is a safe place to share and be. But don't neglect what brings you to this place—the desire to be known and to find meaning for your life. And don't forget that God brings you to this place; you're not a part of your group by chance. Stretch yourself. Dip your feet in the water of honest discussion. Healing can often be found there.

Stay on task. Do you know what TMI is? Too much information. Don't spill unnecessary stuff. Talk-show transparency does little more than bolster ratings and reveal a lack of preparation. If structure isn't your group's strength, then try this approach: Spend a few minutes sharing general comments about the study, and then take each question and give everyone in the group a chance to respond.

While you're listening to others, write down thoughts that their words prompt within you. When you get to the Pray section, listen to each other read prayers aloud. Finally, give time to each person's Live section. What did each of you experience in writing a letter to yourself?

Follow up. Don't let the life application drift away without further action. Be accountable to each other and refer to previous lessons' Live sections often. Take time at the beginning of your group's meeting to review and see how you're doing. Pray for each other between times you get together. Call group members who God brings to your mind and simply ask, "How ya doin'?"

IDENTITY

"It's in Christ that we find out who we are
and what we are living for."
(EPHESIANS 1:11)

Before You Begin

Take just a few moments to still your heart and mind. Remember, God desires to speak to *you* in these moments.

> *You got me when I was an unformed youth,*
> *God, and taught me everything I know.*
>
> PSALM 71:17

READ

Ephesians 1:11-19

It's in Christ that we find out who we are and what we are living for. Long before we first heard of Christ and got our hopes up, he had his eye on us, had designs on us for glorious living, part of the overall purpose he is working out in everything and everyone.

It's in Christ that you, once you heard the truth and believed it (this Message of your salvation), found yourselves home free—signed, sealed, and delivered by the Holy Spirit. This signet from God is the first installment on what's coming, a reminder that we'll get everything God has planned for us, a praising and glorious life.

That's why, when I heard of the solid trust you have in the Master Jesus and your outpouring of love to all the followers of Jesus, I couldn't stop thanking God for you—every time I prayed, I'd think of you and give thanks. But I do more than thank. I ask—ask the God of our Master, Jesus Christ, the God of glory—to make you intelligent and discerning in knowing him personally, your eyes focused and clear, so that you can see exactly what it is he is calling you to do, grasp the immensity of this glorious way of life he has for his followers, oh, the utter extravagance of his work in us who trust him—endless energy, boundless strength!

THINK   *"I took all this in and thought it through, inside and out."* (Ecclesiastes 9:1)

- "It's in Christ that we find out who we are and what we are living for." That sentence might be worth the price of this book. Do you believe it? Reflect on what informs your answer.
- Would you describe your life as "glorious living"? If so, give some details. If not, how would you describe it?

- Reread this passage and underline or highlight the ways Paul
  prays. Do you have anyone in your life who prays for you
  like that? Do you pray in that way for someone else?

READ

From *Between the Dreaming and the Coming True* by Robert Benson[1]

Four

The great risk is not that we will fail to qualify to be reunited with God. The risk is that we will somehow fail to understand why we are here. That we will end up believing that we are being punished because Adam and Eve were barking up the wrong tree. That we will be so fearful of the stories about separating the sheep from the goats that we will end up believing that it is okay to try and have God all to ourselves and shut out those who do not look, act, sound, believe, or worship the way we do. That we will see those stories as the only authentic God stories and put little faith in the ones about hungry prodigals and redeemed tax collectors and Johnny-come-lately yard workers and the lucky sinners brought in to fill up the banquet halls.

We are not here to show something to God. We are here because God — the One who wants to be completely known — has something to show to us.

THINK

"I took all this in and thought it through, inside and out." (Ecclesiastes 9:1)

- What's your initial reaction to Benson's words? Anything that speaks to you and makes you respond "Aha — yes!" or "No way!"?
- Can you think of a time when you were among what Benson referred to as "hungry prodigals, redeemed tax collectors, Johnny-come-lately workers . . . lucky sinners"? What do you think God was showing you during that time?

THINK (continued)

READ

From *The Sacred Romance* by Brent Curtis and John Eldredge[2]

The Message of the Arrows

The deepest questions we ever ask are directly related to our heart's greatest needs, and the answers life gives us shape our image of ourselves, of life, and of God. *Who am I?* The Romance whispers that we are someone special, that our heart is good because it is made for someone good; the Arrows tell us we are a dime a dozen, worthless, even dark and twisted, dirty. *Where is life to be found?* The Romance tells us life will flourish when we give it away in love and heroic sacrifice. The Arrows tell us that we must arrange for what little life there may be, manipulating our world and all the while watching our backs. "God is good," the Romance tells us. "You can release the well-being of your heart to him." The Arrows strike back, "Don't ever let life out of your control," and they seem to impale with such authority, unlike the gentle urges of the Romance, that in the end we are driven to find some way to contain them. The only way seems to be to kill our longing for the Romance, much in the same way we harden our heart to someone who hurts us. *If I don't want so much*, we believe, *I won't be so vulnerable*. Instead of dealing with the Arrows, we silence the longing. That seems to be our only hope. And so we lose heart.

THINK   "I took all this in and thought it through, inside and out." (Ecclesiastes 9:1)

- "Who am I?" "Where do I find life?" How would you respond to these questions?
- Take some time and ponder the voice of love and the voice of shame. Right now, which voice is stronger in your life?

THINK (continued)

READ

From *Telling Secrets* by Frederick Buechner[3]

The White Tower

Genesis points to a mystery greater still. It says that we come from farther away than space and longer ago than time. It says that evolution and genetics and environment explain a lot about us but they don't explain all about us or even the most important thing about us. It says that though we live in the world, we can never be entirely at home in the world. It says in short not only that we were created by God but also that we were created in God's image and likeness. We have something of God within us the way we have something of the stars. . . .

This is the self we are born with, and then of course the world does its work. Starting with the rather too pretty young woman, say, and the charming but rather unstable young man who together know no more about being parents than they do about the far side of the moon, the world sets in to making us into what the world would like us to be, and because we have to survive after all, we try to make ourselves into something that we hope the world will like better than it apparently did the selves we originally were. That is the story of all our lives, needless to say, and in the process of living out that story, the original, shimmering self gets buried so deep that most of us end up hardly living out of it at all. Instead we live out all the other selves which we are constantly putting on and taking off like coats and hats against the world's weather.

THINK   "I took all this in and thought it through, inside and out." (Ecclesiastes 9:1)

- How about you? Have you tried to make yourself into something the world would like better than the way God created you? Think through your reasons for being content or dissatisfied with the way God made you.

- "I ask—ask the God of our Master, Jesus Christ . . . to make you intelligent and discerning . . . so that you can see exactly what it is he is calling you to do" (Ephesians 1:18). Do you think Paul prayed that we would rediscover who God intended us to be? Why or why not?

READ

From *Walking on Water* by Madeleine L'Engle[4]

A Coal in the Hand

My son-in-law, Alan Jones, told me a story of a Hassidic rabbi, renowned for his piety. He was unexpectedly confronted one day by one of his devoted youthful disciples. In a burst of feeling, the young disciple exclaimed, "My master, I love you!" The ancient teacher looked up from his books and asked his fervent disciple, "Do you know what hurts me, my son?"

The young man was puzzled. Composing himself, he stuttered, "I don't understand your question, Rabbi. I am trying to tell you how much you mean to me, and you confuse me with irrelevant questions."

"My question is neither confusing nor irrelevant," rejoined the rabbi, "For if you do not know what hurts me, how can you truly love me?"

THINK

"I took all this in and thought it through, inside and out." (Ecclesiastes 9:1)

- Whoa! What's your reaction to the story of the rabbi? Think about the people who say they love you. Do they know what hurts you?
- Do *you* know what hurts you? Rest assured, that's not an "irrelevant question."

READ

From *The Return of the Prodigal Son* by Henri Nouwen[5]

Claiming Childhood

(Nouwen's reflections take place in the aftermath of an encounter
with Rembrandt's painting **The Return of the Prodigal Son**.)

The younger son's return takes place in the very moment
that he reclaims his sonship, even though he has lost all the
dignity that belongs to it. In fact, it was the loss of everything
that brought him to the bottom line of his identity. He hit the
bedrock of his sonship. In retrospect, it seems that the prodigal had to lose everything to come into touch with the ground
of his being. When he found himself desiring to be treated as
one of the pigs, he realized that he was not a pig but a human
being, a son of his father. This realization became the basis for
his choice to live instead of to die. Once he had come again in
touch with the truth of his sonship, he could hear—although
faintly—the voice calling him the Beloved and feel—although
distantly—the touch of blessing. This awareness of and confidence in his father's love, misty as it may have been, gave him
the strength to claim for himself his sonship, even though that
claim could not be based on any merit.

THINK

"I took all this in and thought it through, inside and
out." (Ecclesiastes 9:1)

- In one way or another, we've each been the prodigal. Think
  back to a time when you left and then returned. What did
  you lose while you were gone? Do you think you lost a certain kind of dignity during that time? Think on this awhile.
- Maybe you're still away from home or the Father or whatever.
  Or maybe you've returned home (literally or figuratively).
  What happened that brought you to your senses?

THINK (continued)

PRAY

Slowly read the following poem a couple of times. What speaks to you? Ask God to bring a word or phrase to the surface. Then allow that word or phrase to begin your prayer. It might seem awkward at first. Fine, let it be awkward. But stick with it.

A Story That Could Be True

If you were exchanged in the cradle and
your real mother died
without ever telling the story
then no one knows your name,
and somewhere in the world
your father is lost and needs you
but you are far away.

He can never find
how true you are, how ready.
When the great wind comes
and the robberies of the rain
you stand on the corner shivering.
The people who go by—
you wonder at their calm.

They miss the whisper that runs
any day in your mind,
"Who are you really, wanderer?"—
and the answer you have to give
no matter how dark and cold
the world around you is:
"Maybe I'm a king."

—WILLIAM STAFFORD[6]

LIVE

These words from Stafford's poem serve as a reminder of this section's theme—*identity*:

> and the answer you have to give
> no matter how dark and cold
> the world around you is:
> "Maybe I'm a king."

You've read from the journal entries, letters, and poems of others. Now it's your turn. What does God want you to live when it comes to *identity*? Use the space below to write a letter to yourself. You might want to date the letter so you can later reflect on where you were and what was going on in your life regarding *identity*.

Date _____

Dear _____

CHURCH

"The church is Christ's body, in which he speaks and acts, by which he fills everything with his presence."
(EPHESIANS 1:23)

Before You Begin

Take just a few moments to still your heart and mind. Remember, God desires to speak to *you* in these moments.

> *I hate all this silly religion,*
> *but you, GOD, I trust.*
>
> PSALM 31:6

READ

Ephesians 1:20-23

> All this energy issues from Christ: God raised him from death and set him on a throne in deep heaven, in charge of running the universe, everything from galaxies to governments, no name and no power exempt from his rule. And not just for the time being, but *forever.* He is in charge of it all, has the final word on everything. At the center of all this, Christ rules the church. The church, you see, is not peripheral to the world; the world is peripheral to the church. The church is Christ's body, in which he speaks and acts, by which he fills everything with his presence.

THINK

"I took all this in and thought it through, inside and out." (Ecclesiastes 9:1)

- Did you notice the C-word in that passage? "At the center of all this, Christ rules the *church.*" Where are you with church right now? Do you see it as central to your life, a confusing necessity, something you can do without, or . . . ?
- Reread what Paul wrote and record your own reflections under these headings:

What I hear Paul saying about church	What I really feel about church

READ

From *An American Childhood* by Annie Dillard[1]

226

> (Note that each entry in this chapter is from a single author,
> Annie Dillard. Look for the progression, from childhood
> to adulthood, in her thoughts on church.)

I quit the church. I wrote the minister a fierce letter. The assistant minister, kindly Dr. James H. Blackwood, called me for an appointment. My mother happened to take the call.

"Why," she asked, "would he be calling you?" I was in the kitchen after school. Mother was leaning against the pantry door, drying a crystal bowl.

"What, Mama? Oh. Probably," I said, "because I wrote him a letter and quit the church."

"You — what?" She began to slither down the doorway, weak-kneed, like Lucille Ball. I believe her whole life passed before her eyes.

As I climbed the stairs after dinner I heard her moan to Father, "She wrote the minister a letter and quit the church."

"She — what?"

THINK   "I took all this in and thought it through, inside and out." (Ecclesiastes 9:1)

- Imagine writing a "fierce letter" saying you're quitting the church. What would you write? If *you* can't write a letter like this, make up an imaginary friend who writes it.

  Dear _____

- Now imagine being the recipient of such a letter—even the one you just wrote. How would you respond? What would you say to the letter writer?

READ

From *Teaching a Stone to Talk* by Annie Dillard[2]

The People

For a year I have been attending Mass at this Catholic church. Every Sunday for a year I have run away from home and joined the circus as a dancing bear. . . .

During the long intercessory, the priest always reads "intentions" from the parishioners. These are slips of paper, dropped into a box before the service begins, on which people have written their private concerns, one by one, and we respond on cue. "For a baby safely delivered on November twentieth," the priest intoned, "we pray to the Lord." We all responded, "Lord, hear our prayer." Suddenly, the priest broke in and confided to our bowed heads, "That's the baby we've been praying for the past two months! The woman just kept getting more and more pregnant!" How often, how shockingly often, have I exhausted myself in church from the effort to keep from laughing out loud? I often laugh all the way home. . . .

A high school stage play is more polished than this service we have been rehearsing since the year one. In two thousand years, we have not worked out the kinks. We positively glorify them. Week after week, we witness the same miracle: that God is so mighty that he can stifle his own laughter. Week after week, we witness the same miracle: that God, for reasons unfathomable, refrains from blowing our dancing bear act to smithereens. Week after week Christ washes the disciples' dirty feet, handles their very toes, and repeats, It is all right—believe it or not—to be people.

Who can believe it?

THINK "I took all this in and thought it through, inside and out." (Ecclesiastes 9:1)

- Reread this excerpt and underline the words or phrases that resonate with you. What about them stirs something in you?
- "It is all right—believe it or not—to be people." Think about your own church. Does it let people be people? What about you?

READ

From *Pilgrim at Tinker Creek* by Annie Dillard[3]

Heaven and Earth in Jest

I live by a creek, Tinker Creek, in a valley in Virginia's Blue Ridge. An anchorite's hermitage is called an anchor-hold; some anchor-holds were simple sheds clamped to the side of a church like a barnacle to a rock. I think of this house clamped to the side of Tinker Creek as an anchor-hold. It holds me at anchor to the rock bottom of the creek itself and it keeps me steadied in the current, as a sea anchor does, facing the stream of light pouring down. It's a good place to live; there's a lot to think about. The creeks — Tinker and Carvin's — are an active mystery, fresh every minute. There is the mystery of the continuous creation and all that providence implies; the uncertainty of vision, the horror of the fixed, the dissolution of the present, the intricacy of beauty, the pressure of fecundity, the elusiveness of the free, and the flawed nature of perfection.

THINK "I took all this in and thought it through, inside and out." (Ecclesiastes 9:1)

- The last sentence in this excerpt contains what Dillard refers to as the implications of living life and welcoming what the future holds. Look back at her list. Do you agree or disagree? Why?
- Dillard's "church" during this time was Tinker Creek. Can you recall a time when some aspect of nature — a creek or mountain or grove of trees — was "church" to you? What did that time mean to you?

THINK (continued)

READ

From *For the Time Being* by Annie Dillard[4]

China

(Dillard is describing aspects of the life of Pierre Teilhard de Chardin,
a Jesuit priest, writer, and paleontologist.)

He ran afoul of Roman authorities over his thinking. . . . Of his
eighteen books, the church permitted only one to see light in
his lifetime, a short scientific monograph published in Peking.
The cardinals were pleased to keep his person, also, tucked
away. They exiled him to China, the second time for virtually
the rest of his life. . . .

Every year, he applied to publish his work; every year,
Rome refused. . . .

Why did he put up with it? One of his colleagues said he
had "the impatience of a prophet." When did he show impatience? His colleagues and many of his friends urged him to
quit the Jesuits. Only for a few weeks, however, did he consider leaving the order. To kick over the traces, he thought,
would betray his Christianity. People would think—perish the
thought—he was straying from the church. His brother Jesuits
defended him and his thinking. Leaving the order would mean,
he decided, "the killing of everything I want to liberate, not
destroy." The Catholic church, he wrote late in life, is still our
best hope for an arch to God, for the transformation of man,
and . . . it is "the only international organization that works."

THINK   "I took all this in and thought it through, inside and
out." (Ecclesiastes 9:1)

- Even if you struggle with the word *Catholic,* use these writings as an opportunity to learn. Reread the last sentence in
the excerpt above. Now write down your working definition
of *church.*

- As you think about your definition of the church, do you think it's still our best hope? Why or why not?

READ

From *Holy the Firm* by Annie Dillard[5]

Part Three

Who shall ascend into the hill of the Lord? or who shall stand in his holy place? There is no one but us. There is no one to send, nor a clean hand, nor a pure heart on the face of the earth, nor in the earth, but only us, a generation comforting ourselves with the notion that we have come at an awkward time, that our innocent fathers are all dead—as if innocence had ever been—and our children busy and troubled, and we ourselves unfit, not yet ready, having each of us chosen wrongly, made a false start, failed, yielded to impulse and the tangled comfort of pleasures, and grown exhausted, unable to seek the thread, weak, and involved. But there is no one but us. There never has been. There have been generations which remembered, and generations which forgot; there has never been a generation of whole men and women who lived well for even one day. Yet some have imagined well, with honesty and art, the detail of such a life, and have described it with such grace, that we mistake vision for history, dream for description, and fancy that life has devolved. So. You learn this studying art history . . . and you learn it, fitful in your pew, at church.

THINK "I took all this in and thought it through, inside and out." (Ecclesiastes 9:1)

- Reread this sentence from the Ephesians passage at the beginning of this Letter: "The church is Christ's body, in which he speaks and acts, by which he fills everything with his presence." Write your reflections on this statement.
- Now reread this sentence by Dillard from the excerpt above: "But there is no one but us. There never has been." Again, record your reflections.

- Do you feel that the apostle Paul and Dillard diverge or intersect? Think through why you've answered this way.

PRAY

Slowly read the following excerpt a couple of times. What speaks to you? Ask God to bring a word or phrase to the surface. Then allow that word or phrase to begin your prayer. It might seem awkward at first. Fine, let it be awkward. But stick with it.

> God does not demand that we give up our personal dignity, that we throw in our lot with random people, that we lose ourselves and turn from all that is not him. God needs nothing, asks nothing, and demands nothing, like the stars. It is a life with God which demands these things.
>
> Experience has taught the race that if knowledge of God is the end, then these habits of life are not the means but the condition in which the means operate. You do not have to do these things; not at all. God does not, I regret to report, give a hoot. You do not have to do these things — unless you want to know God. They work on you, not on him.
>
> You do not have to sit outside in the dark. If, however, you want to look at the stars, you will find that darkness is necessary. But the stars neither require nor demand it.
>
> — ANNIE DILLARD[6]

LIVE

These words from Dillard serve as a reminder of this section's
theme—*church*:

> God does not, I regret to report, give a hoot.
> You do not have to do these things—unless you want to know God.

You've read from the journal entries, letters, and writings of
others. Now it's your turn. What does God want you to live when it
comes to *church*? Use the space below to write a letter to yourself.
You might want to date the letter so you can later reflect on where
you were and what was going on in your life regarding *church*.

Date _____

Dear _____

TRUST

"Saving is all his idea, and all his work.
All we do is trust him enough to let him do it."
(Ephesians 2:8-9)

Before You Begin

Take just a few moments to still your heart and mind. Remember, God desires to speak to *you* in these moments.

> *He's our Savior, our God, oh yes!*
> *He's God-for-us, he's God-who-saves-us.*
>
> PSALM 68:20

READ

Ephesians 2:7-13

Now God has us where he wants us, with all the time in this world and the next to shower grace and kindness upon us in Christ Jesus. Saving is all his idea, and all his work. All we do is trust him enough to let him do it. It's God's gift from start to finish! We don't play the major role. If we did, we'd probably go around bragging that we'd done the whole thing! No, we neither make nor save ourselves. God does both the making and saving. He creates each of us by Christ Jesus to join him in the work he does, the good work he has gotten ready for us to do, work we had better be doing.

But don't take any of this for granted. It was only yesterday that you outsiders to God's ways had no idea of any of this, didn't know the first thing about the way God works, hadn't the faintest idea of Christ. You knew nothing of that rich history of God's covenants and promises in Israel, hadn't a clue about what God was doing in the world at large. Now because of Christ—dying that death, shedding that blood—you who were once out of it altogether are in on everything.

THINK

"I took all this in and thought it through, inside and out." (Ecclesiastes 9:1)

- God has all the time in this world and the next, and he desires to "shower grace and kindness upon us in Christ Jesus." Have you heard this truth a lot in your faith journey? Reflect on what you think it means. What else have you heard of God's desires?
- What do you take for granted in your relationship with Christ?
- What do you have a hard time trusting God with when it comes to your relationship with him?

THINK (continued)

READ

From *Bird by Bird* by Anne Lamott[1]

Introduction

Then a strange thing happened. My father wrote an article for a magazine, called "A Lousy Place to Raise Kids," and it was about Marin County and specifically the community where we lived, which is as beautiful a place as one can imagine. Yet the people on our peninsula were second only to the Native Americans in the slums of Oakland in the rate of alcoholism, and the drug abuse among teenagers was, as my father wrote, soul chilling, and there was rampant divorce and mental breakdown and wayward sexual behavior. My father wrote disparagingly about the men in the community, their values and materialistic frenzy, and about their wives, "these estimable women, the wives of doctors, architects, and lawyers, in tennis dresses and cotton frocks, tanned and well preserved, wandering the aisles of our supermarkets with glints of madness in their eyes." No one in our town came off looking great. . . .

There was just one problem: I was an avid tennis player. The tennis ladies were my friends. I practiced every afternoon at the same tennis club as they. . . .

I thought we were ruined. . . . In the next few months I was snubbed by a number of men and women at the tennis club, but at the same time, people stopped my father on the street when we were walking together, and took his hand in both of theirs, as if he had done them some personal favor. Later that summer I came to know how they felt, when I read *Catcher in the Rye* for the first time and knew what it was like to have someone speak for me.

THINK
"I took all this in and thought it through, inside and out." (Ecclesiastes 9:1)

- What kind of courage do you think it took for Lamott's father to write what he did in the community where they lived?
- Do you think Lamott's trust in her father was undermined or strengthened by the article he wrote and the stand he took? Explain.
- Try to recall an experience similar to Lamott's, where someone else's words or actions brought a certain exposure to your life. Maybe it was an exposure that finally opened your eyes. How did it make you feel?

READ

From *The Safest Place on Earth* by Larry Crabb[2]

It Takes an Armando

(Jean Vanier, founder of L'Arche communities, is commenting here.)

In Rome in 1987, the bishops attending a synod concerned with the role of the laity in the Roman Catholic Church were invited to an unusual gathering. In Vanier's words,

> The Faith and Light communities of Rome invited all the bishops to come to a gathering of their communities, made up of people with intellectual disabilities, their parents and many friends, especially young people. Only a few bishops came. The community of L'Arche in Rome came also, with Armando, an amazing eight year old boy they had welcomed.
>
> Armando cannot walk or talk and is very small for his age. He came to us from an orphanage where he had been abandoned. He no longer wanted to eat because he no longer wanted to live cast off from his mother. He was desperately thin and was dying from lack of food. After a while in our community where he found people who held him, loved him, and wanted him to live, he gradually began to eat again and to develop in a remarkable way.
>
> He still cannot walk or talk or eat by himself, his body is twisted and broken, and he has a severe mental disability, but when you pick him up, his eyes and his whole body quiver with joy and excitement and say, "I love you." He has a deep therapeutic influence on people. . . .
>
> Bishops are busy men. . . . But *someone like Armando* can penetrate the barriers they—and all of us—create around our hearts. . . .
>
> Armando is not threatening. . . . He just says, "I love you. I love being with you."

THINK   "I took all this in and thought it through, inside and out." (Ecclesiastes 9:1)

- Take some time before you answer. Who has been an "Armando" in your life—someone who just loved you and loved being with you, who opened you up merely with his or her presence? Try to articulate what your Armando opened you up to. What did that individual help you see or feel or experience?
- What kind of trust did it take for you to allow your Armando to open your heart? Did you just trust by faith immediately, build trust over a long time, or something in-between?
- What about your faith journey? Did you trust God by faith immediately, build trust over a long time, or something in-between?

READ

From *Amazing Grace* by Kathleen Norris[3]

Church

From the outside, church congregations can look like remarkably contentious places, full of hypocrites who talk about love while fighting each other tooth and nail. This is the reason many people give for avoiding them. On the inside, however, it is a different matter, a matter of struggling to maintain unity as "the body of Christ" given the fact that we have precious little uniformity. I have only to look at the congregation I know best, the one I belong to. We are not individuals who have come together because we are like-minded. That is not a church, but a political party. We are like most churches, I think, in that we can do pretty well when it comes to loving and serving God, each other, and the world; but God help us if we have to agree about things. I could test our "uniformity" by suggesting a major remodeling of the sanctuary, or worse, that Holy of Holies—the church kitchen. But I value my life too much.

I would not find much uniformity, either, if I were to press for agreement on more substantial issues, things that the Christian church has, at times, taught as the truth: Are suicides going to hell? Does divorce diminish a person's ability to be a good Christian? Is the institution of slavery divinely ordained? . . .

At the risk of exposing myself as a terminal optimist, I'd say that things are as they should be. As contentious as we seem to be as a church, we are no less so than the fractious congregations of Corinthians, Romans, Ephesians, and Galatians addressed by St. Paul. Can I consider it a *good* sign—a sign of life—that Christians have continued to fuss and fume and struggle, right down to the present day? It may look awful from the outside, and can feel awful on the inside, but it is simply the cost of Christian discipleship.

THINK   "I took all this in and thought it through, inside and out." (Ecclesiastes 9:1)

- If your pastor read these paragraphs as part of a sermon and then wanted your feedback, what would you say?
- Would your opinion be different if you were giving it to a friend instead of your pastor? Why or why not?
- "It may look awful from the outside, and can feel awful on the inside, but it is simply the cost of Christian discipleship." What do you think of this statement? Do you agree or disagree? Elaborate.

READ

From *Compassion* by Henri Nouwen, et al.[4]

Praying in a Busy World

Prayer requires that we stand in God's presence with open hands, naked and vulnerable, proclaiming to ourselves and to others that without God we can do nothing. This is difficult in a climate where the predominant counsel is "Do your best and God will do the rest." When life is divided into "our best" and "God's rest," we have turned prayer into a last resort to be used only when all our own resources are depleted. Then even the Lord has become the victim of our impatience. Discipleship does not mean to use God when we can no longer function ourselves. On the contrary, it means to recognize that we can do nothing at all, but that God can do everything through us. As disciples, we find not some but all of our strength, hope, courage, and confidence in God. Therefore, prayer must be our first concern.

THINK

"I took all this in and thought it through, inside and out." (Ecclesiastes 9:1)

- Have you ever heard the statement, "Do your best and God will do the rest"? Finish what Nouwen started: Pick it apart and explain why it's a woefully inadequate description of faith.
- Okay, now that you've torn apart this faulty theology, look at your life and think of times when you've fallen prey to it. It might be some significant instance, or it might be something you do nearly every day. Think through and talk with your group about how your experience might look different if you found *all* of your "strength, hope, courage, and confidence in God."

THINK (continued)

READ

From *Markings* by Dag Hammarskjöld[5]

Whitsunday, 1961

(Hammarskjöld is best known for his service as
Secretary-General of the United Nations.)

I don't know Who—or what—put the question, I don't know
when it was put. I don't even remember answering. But at some
moment I did answer *Yes* to Someone—or Something—and
from that hour I was certain that existence is meaningful and
that, therefore, my life, in self-surrender, had a goal.

From that moment on I have known what it means "not to
look back," and "To take no thought for the morrow."

Led by the Ariadne's thread of my answer through the laby-
rinth of Life, I came to a time and place where I realized that the
Way leads to a triumph which is a catastrophe, and to a catastrophe which is a triumph, that the price for committing one's life
would be reproach, and that the only elevation possible to man
lies in the depths of humiliation. After that, the word "courage"
lost its meaning, since nothing could be taken from me.

THINK

"I took all this in and thought it through, inside and
out." (Ecclesiastes 9:1)

- Flip back a few pages and reread Ephesians 2:7-13. Now read
  these paragraphs again. What similarities do you see? What
  differences?
- In terms of your faith, what do you think it means "not to
  look back" and "to take no thought for the morrow"?
- Ponder this statement: "I realized that the Way leads to a
  triumph which is a catastrophe, and to a catastrophe which
  is a triumph." Does that describe your view of your faith
  journey? What kind of trust does it take for you to follow
  God, knowing that both catastrophe and triumph might
  result?

THINK (continued)

PRAY

Slowly read the following poem a couple of times. What speaks to you? Ask God to bring a word or phrase to the surface. Then allow that word or phrase to begin your prayer. It might seem awkward at first. Fine, let it be awkward. But stick with it.

I Did Say Yes

The barely prayable prayer as words fall away,
Words unguessed or unguessable, soft silence only,
Penetrant silence, the pit, then something stirring . . .
Importunate, unquenchable mind, astray
Or aswarm, attuned for odd moments after, then
Drifting. Then a lull & a lifting, then self flickering back,
As the parched sunflower turns toward the sun . . .

A woman kneels, head bent forward, each cell attendant
Upon the flame which, consuming, does not consume,
But gently enwraps, caressing, filling her self with itself,
The burning clouds lingering, then hovering off, like
Mist off a mountain, here in this kitchen, this cell, here,
Where the timeless crosses with time, this chiasmus,
Infinity & now, nowhere & always, this cosmos, this fresh-

Found dimension, all attention gone over now, as flame
Flickers and whispers, all care turning to ash, all fear,
All consequence even, all given over, ah, lover to lover
Now, saying yes, yes, ah, thy will be done, my dear,
Yes echoing down the long halls of time, yes,
In spite of all disappointment, of the death of Love even,
The barely sayable yes again, yes again, yes I will. Yes.

— PAUL MARIANI[6]

LIVE

These words from Mariani serve as a reminder of this section's theme—*trust*:

> In spite of all disappointment, of the death of Love even,
> The barely sayable yes again, yes again, yes I will. Yes.

You've read from the journal entries, letters, and poems of others. Now it's your turn. What does God want you to live when it comes to *trust*? Use the space below to write a letter to yourself. You might want to date the letter so you can later reflect on where you were and what was going on in your life regarding *trust*.

Date _____

Dear _____

CONFIDENCE

"He treated us as equals, and so made us equals."
(EPHESIANS 2:18)

Before You Begin

Take just a few moments to still your heart and mind. Remember, God desires to speak to *you* in these moments.

> *I call to God;*
> *GOD will help me.*
>
> PSALM 55:16

READ

Ephesians 2:16-22

Christ brought us together through his death on the cross. The Cross got us to embrace, and that was the end of the hostility. Christ came and preached peace to you outsiders and peace to us insiders. He treated us as equals, and so made us equals. Through him we both share the same Spirit and have equal access to the Father.

That's plain enough, isn't it? You're no longer wandering exiles. This kingdom of faith is now your home country. You're no longer strangers or outsiders. You *belong* here, with as much right to the name Christian as anyone. God is building a home. He's using us all—irrespective of how we got here—in what he is building. He used the apostles and prophets for the foundation. Now he's using you, fitting you in brick by brick, stone by stone, with Christ Jesus as the cornerstone that holds all the parts together. We see it taking shape day after day—a holy temple built by God, all of us built into it, a temple in which God is quite at home.

THINK

"I took all this in and thought it through, inside and out." (Ecclesiastes 9:1)

- Would you call yourself an "outsider" or an "insider"? Why?
- "You *belong* here." List some words or thoughts that come to mind when you see or hear that phrase.
- Mark or highlight every instance of the word *home* in the passage. What does that word mean to you?

THINK (continued)

READ

From *Staying Put* by Scott Russell Sanders[1]

Two

The word *house* derives from an Indo-European root meaning to cover or conceal. I hear in that etymology furtive, queasy undertones. Conceal from what? From storms? beasts? enemies? from the eye of God? *Home* comes from a different root meaning "the place where one lies." That sounds less fearful to me. A weak, slow, clawless animal, without fur or fangs, can risk lying down and closing its eyes only where it feels utterly secure. Since the universe is going to kill us, in the short run or the long, no wonder we crave a place to lie in safety, a place to conceive our young and raise them, a place to shut our eyes without shivering or dread.

THINK   "I took all this in and thought it through, inside and out." (Ecclesiastes 9:1)

- Look back at your definition of *home*. How does it compare with Sanders' definitions of *house* and *home*?
- Do you think that your faith is more "house" or "home"? Elaborate on your answer.
- If you said "home," do you have a confidence; do you feel "utterly secure"? Where does that confidence come from?

READ

From *Peace Like a River* by Leif Enger[2]

Peeking at Eternity

(Young Davy Land has just been arrested and jailed for shooting two
young men as they were breaking into his family's home. The initial
public response was one of approval.)

Dear Davy Land,

In the Godless day of corrupt youth and permissiveness
toward criminals it is reassuring to see a young man stand up
in defense of hearth and home. That you are reading this in jail
is no surprise to me but instead a sorrowful commentary on
the way we treat those who dare to do what is right. Lest you
begin to doubt yourself let me reassure you. Those fellows who
broke into your house were cast from evil molds, they had in
mind to hurt and kill, and they reaped what they had thought
to sow. Your bravery gives us all new hearts.

THINK   "I took all this in and thought it through, inside and
out." (Ecclesiastes 9:1)

- Can you recall a time when you stood up for your home
  or family in some way? What happened and what was the
  outcome?
- What about a time when you wished you had stood up for
  home or family? Again, what was going on and what was the
  result?
- As best you can tell, did your defense of home or family
  seem to give bravery to the hearts of others? Explain.

THINK (continued)

READ

From *About This Life* by Barry Lopez[3]

Eight

To do this well, to really come to an understanding of a specific American geography, requires not only time but a kind of local expertise, an intimacy with place few of us ever develop. There is no way around the former requirement: if you want to know you must take the time. It is not in books. A specific geographical understanding, however, can be sought out and borrowed. It resides with men and women more or less sworn to a place, who abide there, who have a feel for the soil and history, for the turn of leaves and night sounds. Often they are glad to take the outlander in tow.

These local geniuses of American landscape, in my experience, are people in whom geography thrives. They are the antithesis of geographical ignorance. Rarely known outside their own communities, they often seem, at the first encounter, unremarkable and anonymous. . . . Their knowledge is intimate rather than encyclopedic, human but not necessarily scholarly. It rings with the concrete details of experience.

THINK

"I took all this in and thought it through, inside and out." (Ecclesiastes 9:1)

- Lopez refers to an "understanding of a specific American geography." Do you think people can have an understanding of the geography of faith? Explain what you mean.
- Can you name anyone you know who has an understanding of the geography of faith? Do words like *unremarkable* and *anonymous* describe him or her in any way? If not, choose a few words that do.
- What about you? Do you have an understanding of the geography of faith? How would you describe what that means?

THINK (continued)

READ

From *The Earth Is Enough* by Harry Middleton[4]

Homecoming

(At his father's insistence, the narrator finds himself going to live with
his grandfather and great-uncle in the northern hills
of Arkansas during the Vietnam War.)

There in front of Bate's store the soldier's son retired and the young boy I had never been dared to surface, genuinely thrilled not only to be alive, but just to be. . . . I was suddenly tired of running. I had finally come home. . . .

My grandfather threw my stuff in the back of a dog-weary blue Ford pickup truck, model and year unknown, at least to me. My duffel bag rested on a bed of deer antlers that were as smooth and white as soapstone. He drove and whistled gospel tunes while Albert sat by the open passenger's window tonguing a series of blues riffs, a crescendo of wailing sounds, the notes as pliable as wet willow. Like a boat snug at its moorings, I sat pressed between these two old men, watching the mountain highway flash by through a hole in the floorboard near Albert's feet. I closed my eyes and felt a great wave of relief, a great sense of refuge. My father had given me more than I had hoped. This was more than a hideaway, more than asylum, more than a temporary cloister from a world gone mad. Even as we traveled the narrow road down into the valley below Mount Hebron, I let myself go; I let my mind drift from thoughts of refuge to images of home.

THINK

"I took all this in and thought it through, inside and out." (Ecclesiastes 9:1)

- Think, speak, or write how this excerpt made you feel, what emotions it raised in you.
- Do you recall an experience like the author's — one where you found a sense of "home"?

- Middleton says that he felt safe "pressed between these two old men." Have you ever felt that way in the kingdom of faith? Did these feelings come from people who were or are your mentors? Elaborate.

READ

From *The Wizard's Tide* by Frederick Buechner[5]

Five

(Teddy and Bean are brother and sister; their father is Mr. Schroeder. They are swimming at the beach, and Teddy and his father have decided to swim out to some floating barrels.)

But the best part of the day happened just a little while afterward. Teddy thought the barrels still looked a long way off, and the beach was so far behind he could hardly recognize his mother and Bean sitting on it. His arms were beginning to ache, and he was feeling out of breath. What if he started to drown, he thought? What if he called for help and his father, who was a little ahead of him, didn't hear? What if a giant octopus swam up from below and wrapped him in its slimy green tentacles?

But just as he was thinking these things, his father turned around and treaded water, waiting for him.

"How about a lift the rest of the way?" Mr. Schroeder said. So Teddy paddled over and put his arms around his father's neck from behind, and that was the best part of the day for him and the part he remembered for many years afterward.

He remembered how the sunlight flashed off his father's freckly, wet shoulders and the feel of the muscles working inside them as he swam. He remembered the back of his father's head and the way his ears looked from behind and the way his hair stuck out over them. He remembered how his father's hair felt thick and wiry like a horse's mane against his cheek and how he tried not to hold on to his neck too tightly for fear he'd choke him. . . .

As he swam out toward the barrels on his father's back, he also knew that there was no place in the whole Atlantic ocean where he felt so safe.

THINK "I took all this in and thought it through, inside and out." (Ecclesiastes 9:1)

- Take a moment. Can you recall a time when someone gave you a lift when you didn't think you could make it on your own? Maybe it was a literal lift as in this reading, or maybe it was another kind of support. Write some details about what happened.
- How did this time make you feel? Was there some feeling of safety involved? Try to write out your thoughts.

PRAY

Slowly read the following poem a couple of times. What speaks to
you? Ask God to bring a word or phrase to the surface. Then allow
that word or phrase to begin your prayer. It might seem awkward at
first. Fine, let it be awkward. But stick with it.

Everything Is Going To Be All Right

How should I not be glad to contemplate
the clouds clearing beyond the dormer window
and a high tide reflected on the ceiling.
There will be dying, there will be dying,
but there is no need to go into that.
The lines flow from the hand unbidden
and the hidden source is the watchful heart.
The sun rises in spite of everything
and the far cities are beautiful and bright.
I lie here in a riot of sunlight
watching the day break and the clouds flying.
Everything is going to be all right.

— DEREK MAHON[6]

LIVE

These words from Mahon serve as a reminder of this section's theme — *confidence*:

Everything is going to be all right.

You've read from the journal entries, letters, and poems of others. Now it's your turn. What does God want you to live when it comes to *confidence*? Use the space below to write a letter to yourself. You might want to date the letter so you can later reflect on where you were and what was going on in your life regarding *confidence*.

Date _____

Dear _____

VOICE

"When we trust in him, we're free to say
whatever needs to be said."
(EPHESIANS 3:12)

Before You Begin

Take just a few moments to still your heart and mind.
Remember, God desires to speak to *you* in these
moments.

I've preached you to the whole congregation,
I've kept back nothing, GOD—you know that.

PSALM 40:9

READ

Ephesians 3:7-13

This is my life work: helping people understand and respond to this Message. It came as a sheer gift to me, a real surprise, God handling all the details. When it came to presenting the Message to people who had no background in God's way, I was the least qualified of any of the available Christians. God saw to it that I was equipped, but you can be sure that it had nothing to do with my natural abilities.

And so here I am, preaching and writing about things that are way over my head, the inexhaustible riches and generosity of Christ. My task is to bring out in the open and make plain what God, who created all this in the first place, has been doing in secret and behind the scenes all along. Through followers of Jesus like yourselves gathered in churches, this extraordinary plan of God is becoming known and talked about even among the angels!

All this is proceeding along lines planned all along by God and then executed in Christ Jesus. When we trust in him, we're free to say whatever needs to be said, bold to go wherever we need to go. So don't let my present trouble on your behalf get you down. Be proud!

THINK   "I took all this in and thought it through, inside and out." (Ecclesiastes 9:1)

- "When we trust in him, we're free to say whatever needs to be said, bold to go wherever we need to go." Based on Paul's words, rate your "trust in God" level on a scale from 1 (low) to 10 (high). Are you pleased with your score? Why or why not?
- How do Paul's words make you feel? Do you feel "free" in your faith journey? What about "bold"? Write about that.

THINK (continued)

READ

From *The Heart Aroused* by David Whyte[1]

124

The voice, like the eyes and the face, is traditionally a window to the soul. If, as Gerald de Nerval said, the seat of the soul is not inside a person, or outside a person, but the very place where they overlap and meet with their world, then the voice is as good a candidate as any for getting the measure of our soul life. The voice carries the emotional body of the person speaking. Without verbal explanation, but simply through sound, it tells us *who* is speaking, and, in the meeting room, who has come to work. The voice is as important to our identity as anything we possess. We ask ourselves if we really have a *voice* in this organization, want reassurance that we can *give voice* to our opinions, and if we cannot, speak *soto voce* to those few in whom we choose to confide.

THINK   "I took all this in and thought it through, inside and out." (Ecclesiastes 9:1)

- Remember, Paul wrote, "When we trust in him, we're free to say whatever needs to be said." How do you think that meshes with Whyte's observation: "The voice is as good a candidate as any for getting the measure of our soul life."
- What do you think your voice—the words you use, the emotions behind the words, the truth of what you speak—says about you? What does it say about where you are spiritually?
- Do you feel you have a voice in your relationships (spouse, children, family, friends, church)? Describe that voice. Is it free and bold, as Paul described? Or . . . ?

THINK (continued)

READ

From *A Different Kind of Teacher* by John Taylor Gatto[2]

June 7, 1992

(Gatto is a former New York City and State Teacher of the Year.
His writings reflect an experience in and frustration with
today's educational system.)

Going to the moon didn't really matter, it turned out.

I say that from the vantage point of my fifty-seven years, but also because not long ago I watched as an official astronaut in a silver space suit tried to get the attention of an auditorium full of Harlem teenagers. He came with every tricky device and visual aid NASA could muster, and he was a handsome, well-built black man in his prime with a compelling, resonant voice. Yet the audience ignored him so comprehensively that at several places in his presentation he couldn't continue. It was rude, but I learned something important. . . .

Kids outgrow dolls, even talking ones. It seems likely to me that these kids considered going to the moon a dumb game. I can't verify that because I didn't question them, but most didn't have fathers at all or any dignity in their lives and about half never ate off a tablecloth. What is going to the moon supposed to mean? I couldn't answer that question with any confidence if I were asked, and I had a father, once, and a tablecloth.

THINK   "I took all this in and thought it through, inside and out." (Ecclesiastes 9:1)

- Spend some time thinking before you answer. What are *your* top-five things people talk about that don't really matter? Why?
- Now list *your* five things people talk about that *do* really matter. Why?
- Be honest. Which of the two—don't or do matter—have you spent more time talking about this past week? Can you point to a reason?

THINK (continued)

READ

From *Bird by Bird* by Anne Lamott[3]

200

(Lamott is giving advice to writers on the subject of Finding Your Voice.)

Or maybe truth as you understand it is 180 degrees away — that God is everywhere and we are all where we're supposed to be and more will be revealed one day. Maybe you feel that Wordsworth was right, maybe Rumi, maybe Stephen Mitchell writing on Job. . . .

But you can't get to any of these truths by sitting in a field smiling beatifically, avoiding your anger and damage and grief. Your anger and damage and grief are the way to the truth. We don't have much truth to express unless we have gone into those rooms and closets and woods and abysses that we were told not to go in to. When we have gone in and looked around for a long while, just breathing and finally taking it in — then we will be able to speak in our own voice and to stay in the present moment. And that moment is home.

THINK   "I took all this in and thought it through, inside and out." (Ecclesiastes 9:1)

- Look back at how you described your voice earlier. Is your voice this way because you're avoiding someone or something?
- "Your anger and damage and grief are the way to the truth." Can you think of ways this statement is true? Reflect and elaborate.

THINK (continued)

READ

From *The Language of Life* by Bill Moyers[4]

Robert Bly

(This is taken from Moyers' interview of the poet Robert Bly. Moyers
has asked Bly about the rage and bitterness often found in
William Stafford's poetry. Bly's response contains a poem
of his own sandwiched between commentary.)

Anger comes about when the community and its leaders don't
support the values or people that you love. So I understand
why Bill Stafford's poems could also be angry, even bitter.
I've recently done a long poem which is called "Anger Against
Children," and it's all anger.

Anger Against Children

Parents take their children into the deepest Oregon forests,
And leave them there. When the children
Open the lunchbox, there are stones inside, and a note
    saying, "Do your own thing."
And what would the children do if they found their way
    home in the moonlight?
The planes have already landed on Maui, the parents are
    on vacation.
The mother and father do not protect the younger child
    from the savagery of the others.
Parents don't want to face the children's rage,
Because the parents are also in rage.
This is the rage that shouts at children.
This is the rage that cannot be satisfied.
Because each year more ancient Chinese art objects go on
    display.
So the rage goes inward at last,
It ends in doubt, in self-doubt, dyeing the hair, and love of
    celebrities.
The rage comes to rest at last in the talk show late at night,

When the celebrities without anger or grief tell us that only
the famous are good, only they live well.

I sent that poem to the *Atlantic Monthly* and they wrote:
"We haven't had a poem here in several years that has caused
so much discussion in the office as yours, but we are not going
to print it. Young editors ask, 'Why is this man so angry?'" I
thought, "Well, would the editors say to someone from Bosnia,
'Why are you so angry?'" This analogy is not exact, but our
culture is coming to a place where we don't want to look at
the amount of mistreatment we do toward children. . . . And I
notice, too, often people flying to Phoenix don't want any children on the airplane. They want to water their lawns in peace. I
feel a great sadness over that.

THINK   "I took all this in and thought it through, inside and
out." (Ecclesiastes 9:1)

- Can you recall a time when, as a child, you tried to voice
  a feeling or opinion, only to be raged at by an adult? What
  emotions surface as you think back through that time?
- Have you ever experienced the loss of your voice? Bly wrote,
  "So the rage goes inward at last." Do these words describe
  how you felt? If not, describe your feelings using your own
  words.

READ

From *The Te of Piglet* by Benjamin Hoff[5]

The Upright Heart

(Hoff uses the character Piglet, from A. A. Milne's Winnie the Pooh series, to describe the benefits of being small. In this excerpt, the narrator is having a conversation with Piglet about fear.)

"First of all, the fears that push *you* about are not legitimate, appropriate responses to What Is, such as warnings of danger ahead. Instead, they're the constricting fantasies of What If: 'What if I should meet a Heffalump, or fall on my face, or make an utter fool of myself?' Isn't that true?"

"Yes . . . I suppose so."

"I would suggest that the next time a What If starts badgering you, look it straight in the eyes and ask it, *'All right, what's the very worst that could happen?'* And when it answers, ask yourself, *'What could I do about it?'* You'll find there always will be something. Then you'll see that you can have power in any situation. And when you realize that, the fears will go away."

"They will?"

"Especially when you realize where the power comes from. In one way or another, we're *all* Very Small Animals, and that's all we need to be. So why worry about it? All we have to do is live in harmony . . . and let its power work through us. Let *it* do the work."

"Oh," said Piglet.

THINK   "I took all this in and thought it through, inside and out." (Ecclesiastes 9:1)

- When was the last time you felt very "small"? How did you handle it? Admit it? Fake it? Or . . . ?
- "In one way or another, we're *all* Very Small Animals, and that's all we need to be." What do you hear in those words that relates to your faith journey?

THINK (continued)

PRAY

Slowly read the following poem a couple of times. What speaks to you? Ask God to bring a word or phrase to the surface. Then allow that word or phrase to begin your prayer. It might seem awkward at first. Fine, let it be awkward. But stick with it.

Poetry

I didn't know what to say, my mouth
could not speak,
my eyes could not see
and something ignited in my soul,
fever or unremembered wings
and I went my own way,
deciphering that burning fire
and I wrote the first bare line,
bare, without substance, pure
foolishness,
pure wisdom
of one who knows nothing,
and suddenly I saw
the heavens
unfastened and open.

— PABLO NERUDA[6]

LIVE

These words from Neruda serve as a reminder of this section's
theme—*voice*:

>I didn't know what to say, my mouth
>could not speak

You've read from the journal entries, letters, and poems of
others. Now it's your turn. What does God want you to live when it
comes to *voice*? Use the space below to write a letter to yourself. You
might want to date the letter so you can later reflect on where you
were and what was going on in your life regarding *voice*.

Date _____

Dear _____

FULLNESS

"Live full lives, full in the fullness of God."
(EPHESIANS 3:19)

Before You Begin

Take just a few moments to still your heart and mind. Remember, God wants to speak to *you* in these moments.

> *Oh, thank GOD—he's so good!*
> *His love never runs out.*
>
> PSALM 107:1

READ

Ephesians 3:14-21

My response is to get down on my knees before the Father, this magnificent Father who parcels out all heaven and earth. I ask him to strengthen you by his Spirit—not a brute strength but a glorious inner strength—that Christ will live in you as you open the door and invite him in. And I ask him that with both feet planted firmly on love, you'll be able to take in with all followers of Jesus the extravagant dimensions of Christ's love. Reach out and experience the breadth! Test its length! Plumb the depths! Rise to the heights! Live full lives, full in the fullness of God.

God can do anything, you know—far more than you could ever imagine or guess or request in your wildest dreams! He does it not by pushing us around but by working within us, his Spirit deeply and gently within us.

Glory to God in the church!
Glory to God in the Messiah, in Jesus!
Glory down all the generations!
Glory through all millennia! Oh, yes!

THINK   "I took all this in and thought it through, inside and out." (Ecclesiastes 9:1)

- As you reread this passage, highlight or underline words that speak to you about the fullness of God or the fullness of your relationship with him.
- "God can do anything, you know—far more than you could ever imagine or guess or request in your wildest dreams!" What one thing are you asking God to do these days?
- Do you ever feel like God is "pushing [you] around"? Or is he working within you, with his "Spirit deeply and gently within"? Expand on your thoughts.

THINK (continued)

READ

From *Between Noon and Three* by Robert Farrar Capon[1]

Sticks, Stones, and Snake Oil

(Capon is speaking of the outrageousness of God's grace. Here he is
responding to a reader's concern that he is not serious enough about
morality. The Latin phrase, **loco parentis**, means "in the parental role.")

One footnote. If we are ever to enter fully into the glorious
liberty of the children of God, we are going to have to spend
more time thinking about freedom than we do. The church,
by and large, has had a poor record of encouraging freedom.
It has spent so much time inculcating in us the fear of making
mistakes that it has made us like ill-taught piano students: we
play our pieces, but we never really hear them because our
main concern is not to make music, but to avoid some flub
that will get us in Dutch. The church, having put itself in *loco
parentis,* has been so afraid we will lose sight of the laws of our
nature that it has made us care more about how we look than
about who we are—made us act more like the subjects of a
police state than fellow citizens of the saints.

I have raised . . . six children. After all these years, I now
think my fears that the moral order was always in imminent
danger of collapse were misplaced. My children and I have
spent a great deal of time doing little else than wave it in front
of each other's noses: my lectures to them on truthfulness
were more than balanced by their tirades against me on unfair-
ness. But all the while, there was one thing we most needed
even from the start, and certainly will need from here on out
into the New Jerusalem: the ability to take our freedom seriously and act on it, to live not in fear of mistakes but in the
knowledge that no mistake can hold a candle to the love that
draws us home. My repentance, accordingly, is not so much for
my failings but for the two-bit attitude toward them by which I
made them more sovereign than grace. Grace—the imperative
to hear the music, not just listen for errors—makes all infirmi-
ties occasions of glory.

THINK   "I took all this in and thought it through, inside and out." (Ecclesiastes 9:1)

- "To live not in fear of mistakes." Take this phrase and sit with it a moment. Where does it take you? What thoughts come to mind? Images? Memories? Write them down as best you can.
- If someone asked your best friend, "Does _____ take his/her freedom seriously and act on it?" what would your best friend answer? If you're hard-pressed to answer, you might actually ask your best friend.
- When was the last time you heard the music of grace—really felt God's unmerited favor on your life?

READ

From *Abba's Child* by Brennan Manning[2]

Come Out of Hiding

Thornton Wilder's one-act play "The Angel That Troubled the Waters," based on John 5:1-4, dramatizes the power of the pool of Bethesda to heal whenever an angel stirred its waters. A physician comes periodically to the pool, hoping to be the first in line and longing to be healed of his melancholy.

The angel finally appears but blocks the physician just as he is ready to step into the water. The angel tells the physician to draw back, for this moment is not for him. The physician pleads for help in a broken voice, but the angel insists that healing is not intended for him.

The dialogue continues—and then comes the prophetic word from the angel: "Without your wounds where would your power be? It is your melancholy that makes your low voice tremble into the hearts of men and women. The very angels themselves cannot persuade the wretched and blundering children on earth as can one human being broken on the wheels of living. In Love's service, only wounded soldiers can serve. Physician, draw back."

THINK   "I took all this in and thought it through, inside and out." (Ecclesiastes 9:1)

- In Ephesians 3 at the beginning of this lesson, Paul described the fullness of God that we can experience as "the extravagant dimensions of Christ's love . . . the breadth . . . the depths . . . full lives." How do these words and phrases compare to those in the excerpt from Manning?
- Do you ever think about how God can use your wounds, issues, or problems for his glory? Do you think that living in the fullness of God might mean living with your hurt and pain? Why or why not?

• "In Love's service, only wounded soldiers can serve." Name a few of your wounds. Take some time so you can be honest with yourself. How might God want you to use these wounds to serve him?

READ

From *When The Heart Waits* by Sue Monk Kidd[3]

The True Seed

(Kidd is discussing Meister Eckhart's "true seed"—the living presence of
God's image implanted in the soul.)

I began to get an almost stunning sense of how little attention
we Christians have paid to the soul as the seedbed of divine life
within us. We've mostly looked at it as something to save—an
immortal essence in need of redeeming. How many souls have
you won? then becomes the central question of the Christian
life. But the soul is more than something to win or save. It's
the seat and repository of the inner Divine, the God-image, the
truest part of us.

I woke fresh to the knowledge that the soul is the place
where we meet God. "Here God's ground is my ground and
my ground is God's ground," Eckhart wrote. When I began
to see the soul in this light, the important thing became not
saving the soul but entering it, greening it, developing the
divine seed that waits realization. I realized that the heart of
religion was setting up an honest dialogue with the uniqueness
of one's soul and finding a deeply personal relationship with
God, the inner Voice, the inner Music that plays in you as it
does in no one else.

THINK "I took all this in and thought it through, inside and
out." (Ecclesiastes 9:1)

- How well do you know yourself? If someone said to you,
  "Living a full life is as much about knowing your own soul as
  it is knowing God," what would your response be? Explain.
- What is your response to the last question based on? Your
  upbringing? Personal opinion? Scripture?

THINK (continued)

READ

From *Care of the Soul* by Thomas Moore[4]

Introduction

It is impossible to define precisely what the soul is. Definition is an intellectual enterprise anyway; the soul prefers to imagine. We know intuitively that soul has to do with genuineness and depth, as when we say certain music has soul or a remarkable person is soulful. When you look closely at the image of soulfulness, you see that it is tied to life in all its particulars—good food, satisfying conversation, genuine friends, and experiences that stay in the memory and touch the heart. Soul is revealed in attachment, love, and community, as well as in retreat on behalf of inner communing and intimacy.

THINK   "I took all this in and thought it through, inside and out." (Ecclesiastes 9:1)

- Moore indicates that soul/soulfulness is connected with the particulars of life. Paul wrote that full lives rise out of the extravagant dimensions of Christ's love (see Ephesians 3:18). Do you think these statements intersect or conflict with each other? Why?
- Consider your last experience of "good food, satisfying conversation, genuine friends, and experiences that stay in the memory and touch the heart." Did that experience feel spiritual at the time?
- What's your best memory from this past year? Does it feel spiritual? Why or why not?

THINK (continued)

READ

By Terry Tempest Williams in *Heart of the Land* [5]

Winter Solstice at the Moab Slough

(Williams is writing of her experiences on the Colorado Plateau, Utah.)

I think of my own stream of desires, how cautious I have become with love. It is a vulnerable enterprise to feel deeply and I may not survive my affections. Andre Breton says, "Hardly anyone dares to face with open eyes the great delights of love."

If I choose not to become attached to nouns—a person, place, or thing—then when I refuse an intimate's love or hoard my spirit, when a known landscape is bought, sold, and developed, chained or grazed to a stubble, or a hawk is shot and hung by its feet on a barbed-wire fence, my heart cannot be broken because I never risked giving it away.

But what kind of impoverishment is this to withhold emotion, to restrain our passionate nature in the face of a generous life just to appease our fears? A man or woman whose mind reins in the heart when the body sings desperately for connection can only expect more isolation and greater ecological disease. Our lack of intimacy with each other is in direct proportion to our lack of intimacy with the land. We have taken our love inside and abandoned the wild.

THINK   "I took all this in and thought it through, inside and out." (Ecclesiastes 9:1)

- In the passage at the beginning of this chapter, Paul wrote, "Reach out and experience the breadth! Test its length! Plumb the depths! Rise to the heights! Live full lives, full in the fullness of God." Williams implies that we will experience things such as this if we are "attached to nouns—a person, place, or thing." What nouns are you attached to right now? List as many as you can.

- Do you think that you experience the fullness of Christ's love for you in any of the nouns you listed? Explain, if you can.
- Look back at Williams' words. What's the reason we don't attach ourselves to nouns? The answer might be easy, but it's humbling.

PRAY

Slowly read the following poem a couple of times. What speaks to you? Ask God to bring a word or phrase to the surface. Then allow that word or phrase to begin your prayer. It might seem awkward at first. Fine, let it be awkward. But stick with it.

Allegiances

It is time for all the heroes to go home
if they have any, time for all of us common ones
to locate ourselves by the real things we live by.

Far to the north, or indeed in any direction,
strange mountains and creatures have always lurked:
elves, goblins, trolls, and spiders—we
encounter them in dread and wonder,

But once we have tasted far streams, touched the gold,
found some limit beyond the waterfall,
a season changes, and we come back, changed
but safe, quiet, grateful.

Suppose an insane wind holds all the hills
while strange beliefs whine at the traveler's ears,
we ordinary beings can cling to the earth and love
where we are, sturdy for common things.

—WILLIAM STAFFORD[6]

LIVE

These words from Stafford serve as a reminder of this section's theme—*fullness*:

> we ordinary beings can cling to the earth and
> love
> where we are, sturdy for common things.

You've read from the journal entries, letters, and poems of others. Now it's your turn. What does God want you to live when it comes to *fullness*? Use the space below to write a letter to yourself. You might want to date the letter so you can later reflect on where you were and what was going on in your life regarding *fullness*.

Date _____

Dear _____

WONDER

"But that doesn't mean you should all look
and speak and act the same."
(Ephesians 4:7)

Before You Begin

Take just a few moments to still your heart and mind. Remember, God desires to speak to *you* in these moments.

*The spacious, free life is from God,
it's also protected and safe.*

PSALM 37:39

READ

Ephesians 4:1-7

In light of all this, here's what I want you to do. While I'm locked up here, a prisoner for the Master, I want you to get out there and walk—better yet, run!—on the road God called you to travel. I don't want any of you sitting around on your hands. I don't want anyone strolling off, down some path that goes nowhere. And mark that you do this with humility and discipline—not in fits and starts, but steadily, pouring yourselves out for each other in acts of love, alert at noticing differences and quick at mending fences.

You were all called to travel on the same road and in the same direction, so stay together, both outwardly and inwardly. You have one Master, one faith, one baptism, one God and Father of all, who rules over all, works through all, and is present in all. Everything you are and think and do is permeated with Oneness.

But that doesn't mean you should all look and speak and act the same. Out of the generosity of Christ, each of us is given his own gift.

THINK   "I took all this in and thought it through, inside and out." (Ecclesiastes 9:1)

- Consider your church or small group or home cell or whatever constitutes as your gathering place these days. Does most everyone there "all look and speak and act the same"? Describe that look and speech.
- What about you? Do you have the look? Why or why not?
- Reread these two sentences: "Everything you are and think and do is permeated with Oneness. But that doesn't mean you should all look and speak and act the same." How do you reconcile these two thoughts?

THINK (continued)

READ

From *Lake Wobegon Days* by Garrison Keillor[1]

Sumus Quod Sumus

(Keillor is describing aspects of Lake Wobegon and its citizens,
whose town slogan is Sumus Quod Sumus—"We are what we are."
The Ingqvists are the pastor's family.)

That's why Judy Ingqvist does not sing "Holy City" on Sunday
morning, although everyone says she sounds great on "Holy
City"—it's not her wish to sound great, though she is the leading soprano; it's her wish that all the sopranos sound at least
okay. So she sings quietly. One Sunday when the Ingqvists went
to the Black Hills on vacation, a young, white-knuckled seminarian filled in; he gave a forty-five minute sermon and had
a lot of sermon left over when finally three deacons cleared
their throats simultaneously. They sounded like German
shepherds barking, and their barks meant that the congregation now knew that he was bright and he had nothing more
to prove to them. The young man looked on the sermon as
free enterprise. . . . He wanted to give it all the best that was
in him, of which he had more than he needed. He was opening a Higgledy-Piggledy of theology, and the barks were meant
to remind him where he was: in Lake Wobegon, where smart
doesn't count for so much. A minister has to be able to read a
clock. At noon, it's time to go home and turn up the pot roast
and get the peas out of the freezer.

THINK   "I took all this in and thought it through, inside and
out." (Ecclesiastes 9:1)

- Reread those same sentences that Paul wrote: "Everything
  you are and think and do is permeated with Oneness. But
  that doesn't mean you should all look and speak and act the
  same." With those thoughts in mind, if you were called in
  to advise Judy Ingqvist on whether or not she should sing
  "Holy City" on Sundays, what would you say to her? Why?

- Based on Paul's words, how would you advise the young, long-winded seminarian? Why?
- Again, based on Paul's words, what would you say to the deacons and congregation of this church?

READ

From *The Awakened Heart* by Gerald May[2]

Freedom and Intention

I am encouraging you to let yourself be you and to let God be God. As you touch this gentle permissiveness, you may run into just a little trouble with your religious beliefs. Religious belief is a two-edged sword. It can give us a historically sound foundation and sense of community that make it more possible to relax, to trust God's goodness, and to be more fully in love. But it can also stir up reactions that complicate our simple presence and flood us with mixed messages about the nature of God. So I would suggest this: if religious belief presents some kind of problem for you, don't worry too much about it. Just try to be gently open to your own confusions and love's invitations. . . . Don't worry about whether you are good enough or moral enough to be acceptable in God's eyes.

But do keep your own eyes softly attentive to the truth. Try to be as honest as you can with your experience, and as gentle as possible with yourself. Face into life as it is, into love as it comes. If the Divine is truly divine, you can risk anything for a deeper and truer consciousness of that reality. If not, you really need to take the risk of finding out. Keep coming back to your own common sense and to what you hold most dear, back to the truth of your heart. Let God be God; let the world and other people be who they are; let yourself be yourself.

THINK   "I took all this in and thought it through, inside and out." (Ecclesiastes 9:1)

- What things in life do you "hold most dear"—what things do you love?
- The previous question was a bit of a trick. Now think spiritually. What things in life do you "hold most dear"?

- Compare your lists. In what ways do you live toward those things each day?

READ

From *A Sand County Almanac* by Aldo Leopold[3]

Thinking Like a Mountain

(These are the first two paragraphs in a piece written by Leopold on the occasion of his first wolf kill. In the last paragraph, a "tyro" is a beginner or novice.)

A deep chesty bawl echoes from the rimrock to rimrock, rolls down the mountain, and fades into the far blackness of the night. It is an outburst of wild defiant sorrow, and of contempt for all the adversities of the world.

Every living thing (and perhaps many a dead one as well) pays heed to that call. To the deer it is a reminder of the way of all flesh, to the pine a forecast of midnight scuffles and of blood upon the snow, to the coyote a promise of gleanings to come, to the cowman a threat of red ink at the bank, to the hunter a challenge of fang against bullet. Yet behind these obvious and immediate hopes and fears there lies a deeper meaning, known only to the mountain itself. Only the mountain has lived long enough to listen objectively to the howl of a wolf.

Those unable to decipher the hidden meaning know nevertheless that it is there, for it is felt in all wolf country, and distinguishes that country from all other land. It tingles in the spine of all who hear wolves by night, or who scan their tracks by day. . . . Only the ineducable tyro can fail to sense the presence or absence of wolves, or the fact that mountains have a secret opinion about them.

THINK

"I took all this in and thought it through, inside and out." (Ecclesiastes 9:1)

- Leopold writes that a mountain might be the only one who has lived long enough to listen "objectively" to the howl of a wolf; the premise is that a wolf does hold some value in the economy of creation. Bring that thought into your realm—the place of relationships with family, friends, church, and so on. Have you lived long enough to objectively see the value of the people around you? Or do you still see them for their weaknesses or problems? Explain as best you can.

- What are some ways you could begin to "think like a mountain" each day in those relationships?

READ

From *Arctic Dreams* by Barry Lopez[4]

Prologue
(Lopez writes on the many aspects of life in the Arctic.)

To contemplate what people are doing out here and ignore the universe of the seal, to consider human quest and plight and not know the land, I thought, to not listen to it, seemed fatal. Not perhaps for tomorrow, or next year, but fatal if you looked down the long road . . . and wondered at the considerations that had got us this far.

At the heart of this narrative, then, are three themes: the influence of the arctic landscape on the human imagination. How a desire to put a landscape to use shapes our evaluation of it. And confronted by an unknown landscape, what happens to our sense of wealth. What does it mean to grow rich? Is it to have red-blooded adventures and to make a fortune, which is what brought the whalers and other entrepreneurs north? Or is it, rather, to have a good family life and to be imbued with a far-reaching and intimate knowledge of one's homeland . . . ? Is it to retain a capacity for awe and astonishment in our lives, to continue to hunger after what is genuine and worthy? Is it to live at moral peace with the universe?

THINK "I took all this in and thought it through, inside and out." (Ecclesiastes 9:1)

- Go back and underline or highlight words or phrases that spoke to you in Lopez's writing. Reflect for a while on why the portions you highlighted are meaningful to you.
- A few words have been changed in the following sentences. Read through them and write down how you react.

  "How a desire to put a *human being* to use shapes our evaluation of *him*."

"And confronted by an unknown *person,* what happens to our sense of *security*?"

"Is it, rather, to have a good family life and to be imbued with a far-reaching and intimate knowledge of one's *neighbors?*"

READ

From *My Story as Told by Water* by David James Duncan[5]

Six Henry Stories

My earliest conception of the meaning of the word *wonder* was a feeling that would come over me as a little kid, when I'd picture the shepherds on the night hills above Bethlehem. Even when those shepherds were made of illuminated plastic, standing around in Christmas dioramas on my neighbors' lawns, their slack-jawed expressions of wonder appealed to me. Years later, having become literate enough to read, I learned that those shepherds were also "sore afraid." But—a personal prejudice—I didn't believe in their afraidness. I believed the star in the east smote them with wonder, and that once wonder smites you, you're smitten by wonder alone. Fear can't penetrate till wonder subsides.

Wonder is my second favorite condition to be in, after love, and I sometimes wonder whether there's a difference; maybe love is just wonder aimed at a beloved.

Wonder is like grace, in that it's not a condition we grasp; it grasps us. . . .

Wonder is anything taken for granted—the old neighborhood, old job, old life, old spouse—suddenly filling with mystery. Wonder is anything closed, suddenly opening: anything at all opening.

THINK   "I took all this in and thought it through, inside and out." (Ecclesiastes 9:1)

- Consider the word *wonder.* What images come to mind? Whose voice do you hear? What movie images do you see? What song do you hear? Or . . . ?
- You've probably heard your church or small group pray for revival, renewal, healing, or deliverance. Have you ever heard them pray for wonder?

- Maybe you're convinced this is just a semantic dance. But could wonder be the gift that allows us "to travel on the same road and in the same direction" (Ephesians 4:4) in our journey to God? Reflect on that thought.

PRAY

Slowly read the following poem a couple of times. What speaks to you? Ask God to bring a word or phrase to the surface. Then allow that word or phrase to begin your prayer. It might seem awkward at first. Fine, let it be awkward. But stick with it.

The First Green of Spring

Out walking in the swamp picking cowslip, marsh marigold,
this sweet first green of spring. Now sautéed in a pan melting
to a deeper green than ever they were alive, this green, this life,

harbinger of things to come. Now we sit at a table munching
on this message from the dawn which says we and the world
are alive again today, and this is the world's birthday. And

even though we know we are growing old, we are dying, we
will never be young again, we also know we're still right here
now, today, and, my oh my! don't these greens taste good.

— DAVID BUDBILL[6]

LIVE

These words from Budbill serve as a reminder of this section's theme—*wonder*:

> we also know we're still right here
> now, today, and, my oh my!

You've read from the journal entries, letters, and poems of others. Now it's your turn. What does God want you to live when it comes to *wonder*? Use the space below to write a letter to yourself. You might want to date the letter so you can later reflect on where you were and what was going on in your life regarding *wonder.*

Date _____

Dear _____

FOLLOWING

"But that's no life for you."
(EPHESIANS 4:20)

Before You Begin

Take just a few moments to still your heart and mind. Remember, God desires to speak to *you* in these moments.

GOD rewrote the text of my life
when I opened the book of my heart to his eyes.

PSALM 18:24

READ

Ephesians 4:17-24

And so I insist — and God backs me up on this — that there be no going along with the crowd, the empty-headed, mindless crowd. They've refused for so long to deal with God that they've lost touch not only with God but with reality itself. They can't think straight anymore. Feeling no pain, they let themselves go in sexual obsession, addicted to every sort of perversion.

But that's no life for you. You learned Christ! My assumption is that you have paid careful attention to him, been well instructed in the truth precisely as we have it in Jesus. Since, then, we do not have the excuse of ignorance, everything — and I do mean everything — connected with that old way of life has to go. It's rotten through and through. Get rid of it! And then take on an entirely new way of life — a God-fashioned life, a life renewed from the inside and working itself into your conduct as God accurately reproduces his character in you.

THINK

"I took all this in and thought it through, inside and out." (Ecclesiastes 9:1)

- When Paul talks about this "new way of life" in Christ, what do you think he means? What does it look like?
- What about your story? Did you have to work to get rid of an old life? What did that look like? How is your new life different?
- What "crowd" has the ability to draw you back into old ways of thinking, speaking, acting, feeling? This might be one person or a group, a family member or an actual crowd.

THINK (continued)

READ

From *The Great Omission* by Dallas Willard[1]

Life's Greatest Opportunity

(Willard's book highlights the prevalence of "Christianity"
but the absence of "discipleship"—and he believes
there is a vast difference between the two.)

Concerned to enter that radiant life we each must ask, "Am I a disciple, or only a Christian by current standards?" Examination of our ultimate desires and intentions, reflected in the specific responses and choices that make up our lives, can show whether there are things we hold more important than being like him. If there are, then we are not yet his disciples. Being unwilling to follow him, our claim of trusting him must ring hollow. We could never credibly claim to trust a doctor, teacher, or auto mechanic whose directions we would not follow.

THINK   "I took all this in and thought it through, inside and out." (Ecclesiastes 9:1)

- What do you think the word *disciple* means? Do you consider yourself one of Christ's disciples? Why?
- Reflect on some choices you've made this past week; they might be monumental life choices or just small everyday decisions. Did those choices lead you to be more like Christ or less like Christ?
- Consider those same choices again. Do they reflect something out of the ordinary or do they represent the way you live your life most of the time?

THINK (continued)

READ

From *The Gospel in a Pluralist Society* by Lesslie Newbigin[2]

The Logic of Mission

(This quote by Newbigin helps lead into the excerpt: "The Christian faith is itself an ultimate faith-commitment which can be validated only in its exercise." Michael Polanyi's influence here is one of epistemology, or the study of human knowledge.)

This is a vital question in our present cultural situation where Christian faith is widely regarded as belonging to the world of subjective values rather than to the world of objective facts, and as being therefore merely a matter of personal choice about which the words "true" and "false" cannot be used. . . . Polanyi's answer to the charge of subjectivism is that while we hold our beliefs as personally committed subjects, we hold them with universal intent, to consider and accept them. To be willing so to publish them is the best of our real belief. In this sense missions are the test of our faith. We believe that the truth about the human story has been disclosed in the events which form the substance of the gospel. . . . It follows that the test of our real belief is our readiness to share it with all peoples.

THINK   "I took all this in and thought it through, inside and out." (Ecclesiastes 9:1)

- Write out a few sentences to describe what "sharing your faith" means to you.
- Would your close friends agree with your definitions? Why or why not?
- Newbigin speaks of a "readiness" to share. Does the word *ready* describe you? If not, what other word would you choose?

THINK (continued)

READ

From *Velvet Elvis* by Rob Bell[3]

Welcome

For thousands of years followers of Jesus, like artists, have understood that we have to keep going, exploring what it means to live in harmony with God and each other. The Christian faith tradition is filled with change and growth and transformation. Jesus took part in this process by calling people to rethink faith and the Bible and hope and love and everything else, and by inviting them into the endless process of working out how to live as God created us to live.

The challenge for Christians then is to live with great passion and conviction, remaining open and flexible, aware that this life is not the last painting.

THINK   "I took all this in and thought it through, inside and out." (Ecclesiastes 9:1)

- If your life of following God were a painting, what would it look like? Would it be just started, almost finished, or somewhere in between? Why did you answer that way?
- Where have you been challenged to rethink your faith? Did you initiate this or did someone or something else?

READ

From *In the Name of Jesus* by Henri Nouwen[4]

The Challenge
(L'Arche is a community for mentally handicapped people.)

Now we have to turn to Jesus again because, after having asked Peter three times if he loved him more than the others and after having commissioned him three times to be a shepherd, he said in a very emphatic way:

> "In all truth I tell you
> When you were young
> you put on your belt
> and walked where you liked;
> but when you grow old
> you will stretch out your hands
> and somebody else will put a belt around you
> and take you where you would rather not go"
> (John 21:18)

These words are the words that made it possible for me to move from Harvard to L'Arche. They touch the core of Christian leadership and are spoken to offer us ever and again new ways to let go of power. . . . Jesus has a different vision of maturity: It is the ability and willingness to be led where you would rather not go.

THINK   "I took all this in and thought it through, inside and out." (Ecclesiastes 9:1)

- When it comes to following God, where would you rather not go right now? This might be a literal place or it could be an emotional terrain.
- What's your reason for not wanting to go where God desires to send you?

THINK (continued)

READ

From *When the Heart Waits* by Sue Monk Kidd[5]

Clinging

One morning in my study I looked up the word *clinging*. I discovered that it comes from the Anglo-Saxon word *clingan,* which means "shrink." Sure enough, an undeniable connection exists between clinging and shrinking.

One year I decided to plant English ivy as a border around my flower garden. I dipped the small vines in some pH-balanced enzyme powder and planted them around the flowers. Some weeks later the ivy had grown into a small jungle, clinging around the flower stems and causing the blooms to shrink and shrivel. Standing over my flowers, I understood the deadly effect of clinging.

Now I was beginning to understand its effect on the spiritual life. Clinging creates a shrinking within the soul, a shrinking of possibility and growth.

THINK

"I took all this in and thought it through, inside and out." (Ecclesiastes 9:1)

- Look back over your life. Who or what have you been clinging to? Take some time here.
- Can you point to any areas where clinging has led to a shrinking of your soul?

PRAY

Slowly read the following psalm a couple of times. What speaks to you? Ask God to bring a word or phrase to the surface. Then allow that word or phrase to begin your prayer. It might seem awkward at first. Fine, let it be awkward. But stick with it.

You're blessed when you stay on course, walking steadily on the
road revealed by GOD.

You're blessed when you follow his directions,
doing your best to find him.

That's right—you don't go off on your own;
you walk straight along the road he set.

You, GOD, prescribed the right way to live;
now you expect us to live it.

Oh, that my steps might be steady,
keeping to the course you set;

Then I'd never have any regrets
in comparing my life with your counsel.

I thank you for speaking straight from your heart;
I learn the pattern of your righteous ways.

I'm going to do what you tell me to do;
don't ever walk off and leave me.

— PSALM 119:1-8

LIVE

These words from the psalmist serve as a reminder of this section's theme—*following*:

> You're blessed when you stay on course,
> walking steadily on the road revealed by GOD.

You've read from the journal entries, letters, and poems of others. Now it's your turn. What does God want you to live when it comes to *following*? Use the space below to write a letter to yourself. You might want to date the letter so you can later reflect on where you were and what was going on in your life regarding *following*.

Date _____

Dear _____

PRECONCEPTIONS

"Don't grieve God. Don't break his heart."
(EPHESIANS 4:30)

Before You Begin

Take just a few moments to still your heart and mind.
Remember, God desires to speak to *you* in these
moments.

> *Forget that I sowed wild oats;*
> *Mark me with your sign of love.*
>
> PSALM 25:7

READ

Ephesians 4:26-32

Go ahead and be angry. You do well to be angry—but don't use your anger as fuel for revenge. And don't stay angry. Don't go to bed angry. Don't give the Devil that kind of foothold in your life.

Did you used to make ends meet by stealing? Well, no more! Get an honest job so that you can help others who can't work.

Watch the way you talk. Let nothing foul or dirty come out of your mouth. Say only what helps, each word a gift.

Don't grieve God. Don't break his heart. His Holy Spirit, moving and breathing in you, is the most intimate part of your life, making you fit for himself. Don't take such a gift for granted.

Make a clean break with all cutting, backbiting, profane talk. Be gentle with one another, sensitive. Forgive one another as quickly and thoroughly as God in Christ forgave you.

THINK   "I took all this in and thought it through, inside and out." (Ecclesiastes 9:1)

- "Go ahead and be angry." Did you hear that message growing up? What do you think Paul meant with these words?
- "Watch the way you talk." How about that—was that a warning you received as a child? Was it specific words, tones, attitude? What do you think Paul meant with these words?

READ

From *Wild at Heart* by John Eldredge[1]

The Real Thing

Start choosing to live out your strength and you'll discover that it grows each time. Rich was after some brakes for his car; he called the parts store and they quoted him a price of $50 for the pair. But when he got down there, the guy told him it would be $90. He was taking Rich for a fool and something in Rich was provoked. Normally he would have said, "Oh, that's okay. It's no big deal," and paid the higher price; but not this time. He told the guy that the price was $50 and stood his ground. The guy backed down and stopped trying to rip him off. "It felt great," Rich told me later. "I felt like I was finally acting like a man." Now that may seem like a simple story, but this is where you will discover your true strength, in the daily details of life. Begin to taste your true strength and you'll want *more*. Something in the center of your chest feels weighty, substantial.

THINK

"I took all this in and thought it through, inside and out." (Ecclesiastes 9:1)

- This was written for men. If you're a man, what's your reaction? If you're a woman, what's yours?
- Could you have done what Rich did? Why or why not?
- How do you think this story meshes with Paul's words at the beginning of this lesson (Ephesians 4:26-32)?

READ

From *Nice Girls Don't Change the World* by Lynne Hybels[2]

A Dangerous Woman

I said that the opposite of a nice girl is a good woman. But what I really wanted to say — and what I'm going to say now — is that the opposite of a nice girl is not just a good woman, but a downright dangerous woman. A woman who shows up with everything she is and joins the battle against whatever opposes the redeeming work of God in our lives and in our world.

THINK

"I took all this in and thought it through, inside and out." (Ecclesiastes 9:1)

- "A woman who . . . joins the battle against whatever opposes the redeeming work of God." If you're a woman, do you desire to be this kind of a woman? Why?
- If you're a man, is this the kind of woman you'd want to marry or wish that your wife would become?
- Do you think this kind of woman is rare? Why or why not?

READ

From *Messy Spirituality* by Mike Yaconelli[3]

Notorious Sinners

The Notorious Sinners meet yearly at spiritual-retreat centers, where from the moment we arrive, we find ourselves in trouble with the centers' leadership. We don't act like most contemplatives who come to spiritual-retreat centers—reserved, quiet, silently seeking the voice of God. We're a different kind of contemplative—earthy, boisterous, noisy, and rowdy, tromping around our souls seeking God, hanging out with a rambunctious Jesus who is looking for a good time in our hearts. A number of us smoke cigars, about half are recovering alcoholics, and a couple of the men could embarrass a sailor with their language. Two of the Notorious Sinners show up on their Harleys, complete with leather pants and leather jackets.

THINK   "I took all this in and thought it through, inside and out." (Ecclesiastes 9:1)

- Go back and read Paul's words at the beginning of this lesson. Now read Yaconelli's words again. Are these two passages compatible in any way? If so, how?
- Yaconelli says that some of his friends cuss. In Ephesians 4, Paul cautions about "foul or dirty" words. Do you think Paul was talking about cussing? If so, why? If not, what was he talking about?

READ

From *The Hidden Wound* by Wendell Berry[4]

15

Several months ago I attended the commencement exercises of a California university at which the graduates of the school of business wore "For Sale" signs around their necks. It was done as a joke, of course, a display of youthful high spirits, and yet it was inescapably a cynical joke, of the sort by which an embarrassing truth is flaunted. For, in fact, these graduates were for sale, they knew that they were, and they intended to be. . . . That some of the young women in the group undoubtedly were feminists only made the joke more cynical. But what most astonished and alarmed me was that a number of these graduates for sale were black. Had their forebears served and suffered and struggled in America for 368 years in order for these now certified and privileged few to sell themselves?

THINK "I took all this in and thought it through, inside and out." (Ecclesiastes 9:1)

- "It was inescapably a cynical joke, of the sort by which an embarrassing truth is flaunted." What do you think this sentence means? What would "an embarrassing truth [that] is flaunted" look like?
- Have you ever witnessed something like what Berry speaks about? Be as specific as you can.

READ

From *Remember, I Love You* by Charlie W. Shedd[5]

Rules for a Good, Clean Fight

Major warning here: Cruelty is bad in any form, and of the worst is to throw up to others those things they can never change.

Another weapon to lay aside permanently is overused phrases which have become tiresome: "You are *never* home on time!" "You *always* put the children first!" These and their ilk only ignite fuses and lead to trouble. We will strive to delete "never" and "always" from our battle vocabulary.

THINK

"I took all this in and thought it through, inside and out." (Ecclesiastes 9:1)

- Have you ever considered the words *never* and *always* to be profane talk? Elaborate.
- When was the last time you used those words in a heated conversation? Or had those words used against you? Do you agree that watching the way we talk is about a lot more than four-letter words? Why or why not?

PRAY

Slowly read the following poem a couple of times. What speaks to you? Ask God to bring a word or phrase to the surface. Then allow that word or phrase to begin your prayer. It might seem awkward at first. Fine, let it be awkward. But stick with it.

Words for It

I wish I could take language
And fold it like cool, moist rags.
I would lay words on your forehead.
I would wrap words on your wrists.
"There, there," my words would say—
Or something better.
I would ask them to murmur,
"Hush" and "Shh, shhh, it's all right."
I would ask them to hold you all night.
I wish I could take language
And daub and soothe and cool
Where fever blisters and burns,
Where fever turns yourself against you.
I wish I could take language
And heal the words that were the wounds
You have no names for.

—JULIA CAMERON[6]

LIVE

These words from Cameron serve as a reminder of this section's
theme—*preconceptions*:

> I wish I could take language
> And heal the words that were the wounds
> You have no names for.

You've read from the journal entries, letters, and poems of
others. Now it's your turn. What does God want you to live when it
comes to *preconceptions*? Use the space below to write a letter to
yourself. You might want to date the letter so you can later reflect
on where you were and what was going on in your life regarding
preconceptions.

Date _____

Dear _____

ABANDON

"Watch what God does, and then you do it."
(EPHESIANS 5:1)

Before You Begin

Take just a few moments to still your heart and mind.
Remember, God desires to speak to *you* in these
moments.

*I've made Lord G*OD *my home.*
God, I'm telling the world what you do!

PSALM 73:28

READ

Ephesians 5:1-4

Watch what God does, and then you do it, like children who learn proper behavior from their parents. Mostly what God does is love you. Keep company with him and learn a life of love. Observe how Christ loved us. His love was not cautious but extravagant. He didn't love in order to get something from us but to give everything of himself to us. Love like that.

Don't allow love to turn into lust, setting off a downhill slide into sexual promiscuity, filthy practices, or bullying greed. Though some tongues just love the taste of gossip, those who follow Jesus have better uses for language than that. Don't talk dirty or silly. That kind of talk doesn't fit our style. Thanksgiving is our dialect.

THINK "I took all this in and thought it through, inside and out." (Ecclesiastes 9:1)

- What kind of behavior did you learn from your parents? Good, bad, ugly—list it all.
- The "bad" and "ugly" stuff—have you been able to ditch it? Or is it still hanging around?
- "His love was not cautious but extravagant. . . . Love like that." Wow! What do you think love like that looks like?

READ

From *Little Lamb, Who Made Thee?* by Walter Wangerin Jr.[1]

Summery Jesus Story

(A letter written to Wangerin from Erica Ulrey, a little girl who had read one of his stories. The misspellings are hers.)

Well it all started out when an angle came to mary and told her that she was going to have a baby, and it would be a boy, a boy named jesu. He would be the son of the Lord. They traveled to drusilem. They knocked on inkerp's door but know one had room. So they went to a stable. She had the baby. Jesus grew older when he was 20 or 30. He went and told stories. He got bapties because he wanted to have sins. He told Peater that his enimes would kill him. Jesus arived in drusilem on a donkey. Children were waving palm limes. Jesus went in two the Temple and open the cages of animals tiping taples. His enmies came and hung him up on a cross. After three day's his desiples came to his grave, and angle stood in front of his grave. He was not in the grave. They found Jesus. They thought he was a gost but he had the holes in his hands. Then one day Jesus said I will be up in hevan. The End.

THINK

"I took all this in and thought it through, inside and out." (Ecclesiastes 9:1)

- If you had written this story at age five or six and taken it to your parents, how would they have reacted?
- What was your reaction to the story?
- Do you think God cares if we have every detail correct or does he just want to be in a relationship with us? Or . . . ? Explain your answer.

THINK (continued)

READ

From *Between the Dreaming and the Coming True* by Robert Benson[2]

Three

I know a little girl who claims that she talks with God and that God talks back. She is not the only little one who has ever made such a claim, but she is the only one who has made such a claim around me, so I listen to her. I am afraid not to.

THINK

"I took all this in and thought it through, inside and out." (Ecclesiastes 9:1)

- Did you have someone like Benson in your life as a child? Someone who listened as if you were hearing from God himself?
- Do you think God speaks to us? If so, how does he do it? If you believe this, how can you make sure you're hearing God's voice and not the voice of some imposter?

READ

From *Abba's Child* by Brennan Manning[3]

Come Out of Hiding

The sorrow of God lies in our fear of Him, our fear of life, and our fear of ourselves. He anguishes over our self-absorption and self-sufficiency. Richard Foster wrote, "Today the heart of God is an open wound of love. He aches over our distance and preoccupation. He mourns that we do not draw near to him. He grieves that we have forgotten him. He weeps over our obsession with muchness and manyness. He longs for our presence."

THINK

"I took all this in and thought it through, inside and out." (Ecclesiastes 9:1)

- "He longs for our presence." Do you believe this statement? Why or why not?
- Manning points the finger at *fear* for keeping us from fully knowing God. Would that be the word you'd choose, or another? Explain.

READ

From *The Different Drum* by M. Scott Peck[4]

Chapter XV

(Christian philosopher Beatrice Bruteau is pointing out that
the great revolution in history occurred on Maundy Thursday,
the day before Jesus' crucifixion.)

Until that moment the whole point of things had been for
someone to get on top, and once he had gotten on top to stay
on top or else attempt to get farther up. But here this man
already on top—who was rabbi, teacher, master—suddenly
got down on the bottom and began to wash the feet of his followers. In that one act Jesus symbolically overturned the whole
social order. Hardly comprehending what was happening, even
his own disciples were almost horrified by his behavior.

THINK   "I took all this in and thought it through, inside and
out." (Ecclesiastes 9:1)

- How much of your life has been about getting on top and
  staying there? What kinds of actions have you taken to do this?
- What about getting down on the bottom and serving? What
  kinds of actions have you taken to do this?
- Is this a tension for you? Why or why not?

READ

From *Dangerous Wonder* by Mike Yaconelli[5]

Beyond Carefulness

Truth is, most of us have lost touch with the childlike experience of abandon. We believe in Jesus, we love the idea of Jesus,
we try to do what we believe He wants us to do, but *abandon
everything*? Abandon our job, our security, our nice home, our
parents' expectations for us, our future? Sounds scary. To be
quite honest, abandon sounds irresponsible and crazy.

THINK   "I took all this in and thought it through, inside and
out." (Ecclesiastes 9:1)

- Reflect on your faith journey so far. Has the word *abandon*
  ever come into play? Explain.
- What do you think that word means when it comes to relationship with Christ? How would you define it in your own
  words?
- Do Yaconelli's words resonate with your experience: *scary,
  irresponsible,* and *crazy*? Add a few more words and some
  context to go with them.

PRAY

Slowly read the following poem a couple of times. What speaks to you? Ask God to bring a word or phrase to the surface. Then allow that word or phrase to begin your prayer. It might seem awkward at first. Fine, let it be awkward. But stick with it.

From "For My Father J. Alvin Keen (1899-1964)"

And yet there was the resonance of those elusive harmonies at which
music hints and for which faith strives.
He lived with a growing ability
To deepen the covenants of friendship,
To admire simplicity and dedication,
To accept limitations and disappointments without resentment,
To forgive the unacceptable and trust the unknown,
To love without grasping,
To be grateful for the gift of life.
In his ambience I learned that it is a good thing to take time to wonder.

— SAM KEEN[6]

LIVE

These words from Keen serve as a reminder of this section's theme—*abandon*:

> To love without grasping

You've read from the journal entries, letters, and poems of others. Now it's your turn. What does God want you to live when it comes to *abandon*? Use the space below to write a letter to yourself. You might want to date the letter so you can later reflect on where you were and what was going on in your life regarding *abandon*.

Date _____

Dear _____

REVERENCE

"Out of respect for Christ,
be courteously reverent to one another."
(EPHESIANS 5:21)

Before You Begin

Take just a few moments to still your heart and mind. Remember, God desires to speak to *you* in these moments.

> *Train me in good common sense;*
> *I'm thoroughly committed to living your way.*
>
> PSALM 119:66

READ

Ephesians 5:21-28

Out of respect for Christ, be courteously reverent to one
another.

Wives, understand and support your husbands in ways
that show your support for Christ. The husband provides leadership to his wife the way Christ does to his church, not by
domineering but by cherishing. So just as the church submits
to Christ as he exercises such leadership, wives should likewise
submit to their husbands.

Husbands, go all out in your love for your wives, exactly as
Christ did for the church—a love marked by giving, not getting. Christ's love makes the church whole. His words evoke
her beauty. Everything he does and says is designed to bring
the best out of her, dressing her in dazzling white silk, radiant
with holiness. And that is how husbands ought to love their
wives. They're really doing themselves a favor—since they're
already "one" in marriage.

THINK   "I took all this in and thought it through, inside and
out." (Ecclesiastes 9:1)

- Go back through this passage and highlight the words that
  you find attractive, meaningful, or surprising. Reflect on
  what drew you to those words.
- If you're married, could you share your reflections with your
  spouse? Why or why not?

THINK (continued)

READ

From *A Year by The Sea* by Joan Anderson[1]

September

A relationship to me was supposed to be about adventure, having fun, sharing. He saw his primary role as breadwinner and occasional participant in the periphery of our family life. I would fill the weekends with people and parties, hoping to ignite his spirit, but often such occasions made him retreat all the more. When I would try to pry him out of his shell, his retort would be "When will you ever be satisfied with what is? If it's excitement you want, then go get it!"

So I did, promptly developing a crush on a married man—running away from the intensity of those feelings to a writer's conference in Maine, returning with new contacts to energize my career, signing up book projects, thus burying my personal needs in the glamour of the writing profession. Although each escapade offered momentary titillation, all of them failed to bring me what I craved—intimacy and relatedness.

THINK   "I took all this in and thought it through, inside and out." (Ecclesiastes 9:1)

- Based on what you read about Anderson's thoughts in this excerpt, imagine how she might respond to Paul's words at the beginning of this lesson (Ephesians 5:21-28). Come up with a few statements or questions she'd have for Paul.
- If someone said to you, "When will you ever be satisfied with what is? If it's excitement you want, then go get it," how would you react? Explain.

THINK (continued)

READ

From *Ragman and Other Cries of Faith* by Walter Wangerin Jr.[2]

Fights Unfought, Forgiveness Forgone

(Thanne is Wangerin's wife. The episode is from
the early days of marriage.)

We used to fight, Thanne and I.

Well, it was always a "sort-of" fight, on account of, it was all one-sided. I did the talking. She did the not-talking. And then what she did was, she would cry.

I would say, "Thanne, what's the matter?" Real sympathy in my voice, you understand. And caring and gentleness in abundance, and great-hearted love. Dog-eyed solicitation: "Oh, Thanne, what is the matter?"

And she would only cry.

So then, I had my second strategem. So then, I would sigh loudly in order to indicate that I have troubles, too, not the least of which is an uncommunicative wife—and how are we going to solve anything if we don't *say* anything? (I was skilled at the sophisticated sigh.) And I would ask again, allowing just a tad of aggravation to bite my voice, "What *is* the matter, Thanne?"

THINK "I took all this in and thought it through, inside and out." (Ecclesiastes 9:1)

- Ponder this scenario and talk it out with your group. Flesh out "what's the matter."
- Reread Ephesians 5:21-28 at the beginning of the lesson. Would you say that Wangerin or his wife treated each other with reverence? What could each have done differently?

THINK (continued)

READ

From *Crossing to Safety* by Wallace Stegner[3]

13

> (Sally is the narrator's wife. Wizard is their horse. They have
> just witnessed a verbal standoff between their married
> friends, Sid and Charity. Charity won. Charity always wins.)

Sally and I walk the trail that the two ahead have made through
the wet grass. . . . Her eyes flash up, her lip curls. "Wasn't she
preposterous? But she knows it. She's sorry."

"She ought to be."

Sally stops, and Wizard, walking in his sleep, almost runs
over us. "Larry, let's not let it spoil things. It'll blow over. It
already has."

"She acts like his mother, not his wife. If she'd treat him
the way she treats, for instance, you and me, everything would
be dandy."

THINK   "I took all this in and thought it through, inside and
          out." (Ecclesiastes 9:1)

- Again, think through this scenario and talk it over with your
  group. Just let your conversation run.
- Do the same exercise. Reread Ephesians 5:21-28 at the
  beginning of the lesson. There are two couples in this
  excerpt—how did the various players do when it comes to
  reverence?

THINK (continued)

READ

From *Peace Like a River* by Leif Enger[4]

Winning Her Hand

(Reuben Land narrates, Jeremiah is his father, and Swede is his sister. Jeremiah's first wife died and after many years, he is now courting Roxana.)

He really did look good, a clean-shaven courting man with quick arms and steady eyes. He had to know that Roxana loved him already, but he wouldn't have me pointing it out. Who could blame him? No doubt Dad had thought his pursuing days long over. Why sprint through such sweet country? How often does a man get to use phrases like "winning her hand"? And it wasn't just talk; he truly meant to win it. He set himself toward her like an athlete. He slept in the cold trailer and spent most of each day there. He stopped entering the house casually. He knocked for admittance. Swede and I missed his constant presence, yet when he arrived the very light seemed to change—like light bouncing in off June maples. And Roxana, always lovely now, Roxana at his knock would look around at Swede and me as though all this were as unnecessary as it was wonderful, and she'd go to the door and there Dad would be in his best clothes, suit coat, often a hothouse carnation in hand. He assumed nothing.

THINK
"I took all this in and thought it through, inside and out." (Ecclesiastes 9:1)

- One last time, okay? Think through this scenario and talk it over with your group.
- And again, reread Ephesians 5:21-28 at the beginning of the lesson. A lot of characters here—which one resonates with you? How did that character handle what Paul wrote about reverence?

THINK (continued)

PRAY

Slowly read the following poem a couple of times. What speaks to you? Ask God to bring a word or phrase to the surface. Then allow that word or phrase to begin your prayer. It might seem awkward at first. Fine, let it be awkward. But stick with it.

When We Walked Together—For Eileen

When we walked together
in the cool of the evening,
walked together, you and I,
in the cool of the evening,
after the heat of the day,
after the long hours under the sweating sun,
after the buzzing words like black flies
had at long last ceased their querulous stinging,
after the questions, after the answers
that refused at last to answer anything at all,
in the cool of the evening, when we walked
in the garden, you and I, in the cool of the evening.
When it was no longer important
for either of us to speak, since the words,
whatever words they might have been,
would have been beside the point,
would have said nothing our hearts
did not already know, where simply being there,
there in the cool of the evening
was all that finally mattered,
with the long night coming on, and the last trill
of birdsong fading off in the distance
by the ridge of the tree line,
when we walked together there in the garden,
in the cool of the evening, you and I.

— PAUL MARIANI[5]

LIVE

These words from Mariani serve as a reminder of this section's theme —*reverence*:

since the words,
whatever words they might have been,
would have been beside the point

You've read from the journal entries, letters, and poems of others. Now it's your turn. What does God want you to live when it comes to *reverence*? Use the space below to write a letter to yourself. You might want to date the letter so you can later reflect on where you were and what was going on in your life regarding *reverence*.

Date _____

Dear _____

NO RULES, JUST WRITE

"God is strong, and he wants you strong."
(EPHESIANS 6:10)

Before You Begin

Take just a few moments to still your heart and mind. Remember, God desires to speak to *you* in these moments.

Real help comes from GOD.

PSALM 3:8

READ

Ephesians 6:10-18

And that about wraps it up. God is strong, and he wants you strong. So take everything the Master has set out for you, well-made weapons of the best materials. And put them to use so you will be able to stand up to everything the Devil throws your way. This is no afternoon athletic contest that we'll walk away from and forget about in a couple of hours. This is for keeps, a life-or-death fight to the finish against the Devil and all his angels.

Be prepared. You're up against far more than you can handle on your own. Take all the help you can get, every weapon God has issued, so that when it's all over but the shouting you'll still be on your feet. Truth, righteousness, peace, faith, and salvation are more than words. Learn how to apply them. You'll need them throughout your life. God's Word is an *indispensable* weapon. In the same way, prayer is essential in this ongoing warfare. Pray hard and long. Pray for your brothers and sisters. Keep your eyes open. Keep each other's spirits up so that no one falls behind or drops out.

\ \ \ \

You've walked through Paul's letter to the Ephesians. You've also walked through journal entries, letters, and poems from other pilgrims along the way. Now it's your turn. The challenge before you is to write three letters to three friends. These could include your spouse, an uncle you haven't spoken to for years, a former teacher, or your best friend from grade school. Go back through the lessons and allow God's Spirit to remind you of particularly meaningful places in Ephesians, journal entries that resonated with you, or poems that touched you deeply. Then allow time for the faces of those family or friends to sur-

LETTER 12 / 169

face alongside those words.

Give this some time. If you build the space, they will come.

Just a side note: You don't have to limit your recipients to those who are living. You might write a letter to a grandparent who passed away or a soldier who died in harm's way. At times, writing to those who have gone on can open the door to significant growth and healing in our lives.

Then sit down with paper and pencil, or keyboard and screen, and share some of the thoughts and feelings that come to the surface. This might seem to be an unorthodox way to finish. But remember, this isn't a Bible study. The letters you send carry the possibility of witness, a way to invite soulfulness in a soul-less world. May they prompt reflection in another heart, honor the always-appropriate gift of memory, and speak truths of the past into today and eternity.

\ \ \ \

As you begin your letters (but end this book), ground your intentions by filling in three names.

Dear _____.

Dear _____.

Dear _____.

NOTES

LETTER 1: **IDENTITY**

1. Robert Benson, *Between the Dreaming and the Coming True* (New York: Tarcher/Putnam, 1996), 68.
2. Brent Curtis and John Eldredge, *The Sacred Romance: Drawing Closer to the Heart of God* (Nashville: Nelson, 1997), 32–33.
3. Selection from pages 44–45 from *Telling Secrets* by Frederick Buechner. Copyright © 1991 by Frederick Buechner. Reprinted by permission of HarperCollins Publishers.
4. Madeleine L'Engle, *Walking On Water: Reflections on Faith & Art* (Wheaton, IL: Harold Shaw Publishers, 1980), 70–71.
5. Henri Nouwen, *The Return of the Prodigal Son: A Story of Homecoming* (New York: Image Books, 1994), 49.
6. "A Story That Could Be True," copyright 1960, 1970, 1977, 1982, 1998 by the Estate of William Stafford. Reprinted from *The Way It Is: New & Selected Poems* with the permission of Graywolf Press, Saint Paul, Minnesota.

LETTER 2: **CHURCH**

1. Annie Dillard, *An American Childhood* (New York: Harper & Row, 1987), 226.
2. Selection from pages 19–20 from *Teaching a Stone to Talk: Expeditions and Encounters* by Annie Dillard. Copyright © 1982 by Annie Dillard. Reprinted by permission of HarperCollins Publishers.
3. Annie Dillard, *Pilgrim at Tinker Creek* (New York: HarperPerennial, 1974), 2–3.

4. Annie Dillard, *For the Time Being* (New York: Vintage Books, 1999), 102–104.

5. Annie Dillard, *Holy the Firm* (New York: Harper & Row, 1977), 56–57.

6. Dillard, *Teaching a Stone to Talk*, 31.

LETTER 3: **TRUST**

1. Anne Lamott, *Bird by Bird: Some Instructions on Writing and Life* (New York: Anchor Books, 1995), xviii–xix.

2. Larry Crabb, *The Safest Place on Earth* (Nashville: Word, 1999), 29–30. Excerpt from *From Brokenness to Community* by Jean Vanier, copyright © 1992 by Paulist Press, Inc. New York/Mahwah, NJ. Reprinted by permission of Paulist Press, Inc. www.paulistpress.com.

3. Kathleen Norris, *Amazing Grace: A Vocabulary of Faith* (New York: Riverhead Books, 1998), 272.

4. Donald P. McNeill, Douglas A Morrison, Henri J. M. Nouwen, *Compassion: A Reflection on the Christian Life* (Garden City, NY: Doubleday, 1982), 104.

5. Dag Hammarskjöld, *Markings,* trans. Leif Sjoberg and W. H. Auden (New York: Ballantine, 1964), 180.

6. *Deaths & Transfigurations* by Paul Mariani, copyright © 2005 by Paul Mariani. Used by permission of Paraclete Press. www.paracletepress.com, 1-800-451-5006.

LETTER 4: **CONFIDENCE**

1. Scott Russell Sanders, *Staying Put: Making a Home in a Restless World* (Boston: Beacon Press, 1993), 29.

2. Leif Enger, *Peace Like a River* (New York: Grove Press, 2001), 60.

3. Barry Lopez, *About This Life: Journeys on the Threshold of Memory* (New York: Knopf, 1998), 132–133.

4. Harry Middleton, *The Earth Is Enough: Growing Up in a World of Flyfishing, Trout, & Old Men* (Boulder, CO: Pruett Publishing, 1996), 40–42.

5. Frederick Buechner, *The Wizard's Tide: A Story* (New York: HarperCollins, 1990), 45–46.

6. By kind permission of the author and The Gallery Press, Lougherew, Oldcastle, County Meath, Ireland from *Collected poems* (1999).

LETTER 5: **VOICE**

1. David Whyte, *The Heart Aroused: Poetry and the Preservation of the Soul in Corporate America* (New York: Doubleday Dell, 1994), 124–125.
2. John Taylor Gatto, *A Different Kind of Teacher: Solving the Crisis of American Schooling* (Berkeley, CA: Berkeley Hill Books, 2001), 200–201.
3. Anne Lamott, *Bird by Bird: Some Instructions on Writing and Life* (New York: Anchor Books, 1994), 200–201.
4. Bill Moyers, *The Language of Life: A Festival of Poets* (New York: Doubleday, 1995), 65–66.
5. Benjamin Hoff, *The Te of Piglet* (New York: Penguin Books, 1992), 204–205.
6. From "Poetry" from *Selected Poems* by Pablo Neruda, translated by Alasdair Reid, edited by Nathaniel Tarn, and published by Jonathan Cape. Reprinted by permission of The Random House Group, Ltd.

LETTER 6: **FULLNESS**

1. Robert Farrar Capon, *Between Noon and Three: Romance, Law and the Outrage of Grace (4222)*, copyright © 1997 Wm. B. Eerdmans Publishing Company, Grand Rapids, Michigan. Reprinted by permission of the publisher, all rights reserved.
2. Brennan Manning, *Abba's Child: The Cry of the Heart for Intimate Belonging* (Colorado Springs: NavPress, 1994), 24–25.
3. Sue Monk Kidd, *When the Heart Waits: Spiritual Direction for Life's Sacred Questions* (New York: Harper, 1990), 48.
4. Thomas Moore, *Care of the Soul: A Guide for Cultivating Depth and Sacredness in Everyday Life* (New York: HarperCollins, 1992), introduction.
5. Terry Tempest Williams in *Heart of the Land: Essays on Last Great Places*, Joseph Barbato and Lisa Weinerman, eds. (New York: Vintage Books, 1994), 4–5.

6. "Allegiances," copyright 1960, 1970, 1977, 1982, 1998 by the Estate of William Stafford. Reprinted from *The Way It Is: New & Selected Poems* with the permission of Graywolf Press, Saint Paul, Minnesota.

LETTER 7: **WONDER**

1. Garrison Keillor, *Lake Wobegon Days* (New York: Viking, 1985), 96–97.
2. Excerpt from page 57 from *The Awakened Heart* by Gerald G. May, MD. Copyright © 1991 by Gerald G. May, MD. Reprinted by permission of HarperCollins Publishers.
3. Aldo Leopold, *A Sand County Almanac: And Sketches Here and There* (New York: Oxford University Press, 1949), 129.
4. Barry Lopez, *Arctic Dreams: Imagination and Desire in a Northern Landscape* (New York: Bantam Books, 1986), 13–14.
5. David James Duncan, *My Story as Told by Water* (San Francisco: Sierra Club Books, 2001), 88–89.
6. In *Good Poems,* selected and introduced by Garrison Keillor (New York: Penguin Books, 2002), 428.

LETTER 8: **FOLLOWING**

1. Dallas Willard, *The Great Omission: Reclaiming Jesus's Essential Teachings on Discipleship* (New York: HarperCollins, 2006), 11.
2. Lesslie Newbigin, *The Gospel in a Pluralist Society* (Grand Rapids: Eerdmans, 1989), 126.
3. Rob Bell, *Velvet Elvis: Repainting the Christian Faith* (Grand Rapids: Zondervan, 2005), 10–11.
4. Henri Nouwen, *In the Name of Jesus: Reflections on Christian Leadership* (New York: Crossroad, 2001), 61–62.
5. Sue Monk Kidd, *When the Heart Waits: Spiritual Direction for Life's Sacred Questions* (New York: HarperCollins, 1990), 105.

LETTER 9: **PRECONCEPTIONS**

1. John Eldredge, *Wild at Heart: Discovering the Passionate Soul of a Man* (Nashville: Nelson, 2001), 147.
2. Lynne Hybels, *Nice Girls Don't Change the World* (Grand Rapids: Zondervan, 2005), 89.

3. Mike Yaconelli, *Messy Spirituality: God's Annoying Love for Imperfect People* (Grand Rapids: Zondervan, 2002), 16.
4. Wendell Berry, *The Hidden Wound* (San Francisco: North Point Press, 1989), 128.
5. Charlie W. Shedd, *Remember, I Love You: Martha's Story* (New York: HarperCollins, 1990), 41.
6. Julia Cameron, in *The Artist's Way: A Spiritual Path to Higher Creativity* (New York: Jeremy P Tarcher/Putnam, 1992), 204.

LETTER 10: **ABANDON**

1. Walter Wangerin Jr., *Little Lamb, Who Made Thee?* (Grand Rapids: Zondervan, 1993), 79.
2. Robert Benson, *Between the Dreaming and the Coming True* (New York: Tarcher/Putnam, 1996), 43.
3. Brennan Manning, *Abba's Child: The Cry of the Heart for Intimate Belonging* (Colorado Springs: NavPress, 1994), 16.
4. M. Scott Peck, *The Different Drum: Community Making and Peace* (New York: Touchstone, 1987), 293–294.
5. Mike Yaconelli, *Dangerous Wonder: The Adventure of Childlike Faith* (Colorado Springs: NavPress, 2003), 57.
6. Sam Keen, *Apology for Wonder* (New York: Harper & Row, 1969), 7.

LETTER 11: **REVERENCE**

1. Joan Anderson, *A Year by the Sea: Thoughts of an Unfinished Woman* (New York: Broadway Books, 1999), 5.
2. Walter Wangerin Jr., *Ragman and Other Cries of Faith* (New York: Harper, 1994), 124–125.
3. Wallace Stegner, *Crossing to Safety* (New York: Penguin Books, 1987), 185.
4. Leif Enger, *Peace Like a River* (New York: Grove Press, 2001), 253–254.
5. Paul Mariani, *Deaths & Transfigurations: Poems* (Brewster, MA: Paraclete Press, 2005), 92.

DIG INTO GOD'S WORD WITH THESE GREAT BIBLE STUDIES.

Living the Letters: Galatians
The Navigators
ISBN-13: 978-1-60006-029-8
ISBN-10: 1-60006-029-3

In a modern world filled with text messages, e-mails, and PDAs, the fine art of written correspondence has been replaced by convenience. A handwritten letter takes time, indicating a thoughtful and purposeful statement that lives long after it's crafted. This unique twelve-week Bible study encourages readers to contemplate Paul's carefully chosen words of counsel while exploring the rich truths contained within the text.

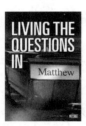
Living the Questions in Matthew
The Navigators
ISBN-13: 978-1-57683-833-4
ISBN-10: 1-57683-833-1

Many believers think of Jesus as the man with all the answers, sent down to earth to tell us everything we need to know. So why are we still left with so many nagging questions we never seem to find answers for? This study of the gospel of Matthew, using *The Message*—the eye-opening translation by Eugene Peterson—will help you embrace life's questions and build a stronger faith.

Living the Questions in Luke
The Navigators
ISBN-13: 978-1-57683-861-7
ISBN-10: 1-57683-861-7

This thought-provoking study of the gospel of Luke will help readers wrestle personally with the often-unsettling questions Jesus asked. Includes text from *The Message*, along with real-life anecdotes and excerpts from literature, pop culture, and current events.